Riding Bike in the Fifties

Albert Drake

Flat Out Press

Acknowledgements

Sections of the long poem, Riding Bike, were published in the following magazines: *Asphalt, Back Door, Coe Review, Easy Rider, Happiness Holding Tank, Karaki* and *Salt Lick*.
A section was published in *The Bikers* (England), Mazz Harris, editor.
A chapbook, *Riding Bike in the Fifties* (Stone Press), was published in 1973.
A shorter version was pirated by inmates at Folsom Prison and published by Zetetic Press, 1974.
The following essays first appeared in *Goodguys Gazette*:
"My First Motorcycle," "Chaos," "Choices," "Incident" and "Going Down."
"Cruising on a Vespa at Midcentury" first appeared in a different form, in *American Scooterist* and *Kickstart*.
All are used with permission.

©2012 Albert Drake
Layout and text improvements by Linda Candello

ISBN: 0-936892-27-7
Printed in U.S.A.

Flat Out Press
P.O. Box 66874
Portland, OR 97290-6874

www.flatoutpress.com

All rights reserved. No part of this book may be reproduced or transmitted in any form or by any means, electronic or mechanical, including photography, recording or any information storage and retrieval system, without prior permission from the publisher, except by a reviewer who may quote brief passages in review.
Notice: The information in this book is true and complete to the best of our knowledge. It is offered without guarantee on the part of the author and Flat Out Press. The author and publisher disclaim all liability in connection with the content of this book.

Table of Contents

Introduction 1
My First Motorcycle 5
Johnny Payne 11
Merhar's Drive-In 15
Who Rode 18
Cliff Majhor 21
Where We Rode 27
Sensations 32
Chaos 35
What We Wore 39
The Morning Speed Run 42
Paul Watts 45
Incident 49
What We Rode 54
Gary Davis 57
Bill Zerbach 61
Sidewinders 67
What We Hated 74
What We Loved 74
On Seeing the Wild One 75
Dealers and Shops 77
Elden Wright 81
Choices 85
Cut Downs 91
Getting Home 93
Three-Wheeling 101
Impressions 105
Mark Budlong 111
On Being the Wild One 120
Going Down 123
Cruising on a Vespa at Midcentury 127

A speedway bike with JAP engine.

Introduction

Sometimes, on certain mornings in early fall, when there is a light fog and the air holds a hint of moisture, I can recall so clearly the sound of a single's exhaust. The mist put a layer of moisture on the chrome, and I'd wipe dew off the seat with a rag, tickle the carb and mount the bike. Using the compression release, I'd kick the piston through until it was on compression stroke and kick it without the compression release, maybe once, maybe more, until it fired. The exhaust was crisp, sharp, with a bark as I cracked the throttle.

I'd let the oil flow, engine warm, then click the shift lever into low, and everything felt tight, precise. Idling through the neighborhood in first, then second, I felt the air pass over me and when I got into third gear I felt alive. On Foster Road I'd stop, swing right and accelerate through the gears, in no hurry to get anywhere. I'd get into fourth gear by the time I had to start slowing for the blinking light at 92nd. I'd let the exhaust back off and as it began to mellow I'd kick the bike into third. I had a high pipe, and a previous owner had added over a foot of aluminum tubing as an extension. The result was an exhaust with a sharp sound, especially on deceleration; I'd made a snuffy which I could quickly shove in the end of the pipe, which reduced the exhaust sound to anemic whisper but I loved the noise of the bare exhaust, and as I decelerated it would rise then fall, gear by gear, stretching to the final notes until I shifted down to first, and then I'd do it all over again. It was the sound of being alive!

I rode a motorcycle because my father rode one. It was his way of dealing with the frustrations of hard work, paying bills, trying to get ahead, broken machines, feeling punk. Riding a motorcycle was the closest thing my father had to a hobby. He didn't hunt or fish, garden or fool with radios. He didn't collect anything. He didn't travel. That's not to say that he wouldn't have liked to do those things, it's just that he never had the time or money. He never even took a vacation, not in the way that people do today. Our idea of a vacation was to get the big tent my parents had bought when they arrived in Portland by train, put it in the trunk of my father's sedan and drive up an old logging road in the Tillamook Burn and spend a long weekend roughing it. If he had taken a longer vacation it would have meant that he wasn't working, and every day off the job meant that much less income. If he had had more money everything would have been different.

He grew up in North Dakota, and had all manner of machines, including a snow mobile that he built himself from cast-off automotive parts. He had the ability to drive any machine, from motorcycles to dump trucks to bulldozers and steam shovels. He was an able mechanic and made repairs on all those rigs. He loved the topography of Oregon, to go uphill and down, and he loved speed. Before WW II he took me to the midget races at Jantzen Beach. From somewhere I got the idea that he had an opportunity to drive a midget in a race, or so I told the guys at school, but he never did.

Introduction

Because he had a bad heart he was exempt from the draft, and during the war he drove a whirly crane in the Oregon and Swan Island shipyards, sitting in that cabin a hundred feet in the air, lifting huge sheets of steel. He had a sense of adventure and seemed not to know the meaning of fear. On one occasion he had to go to Salem on business and normally he would have driven there in an hour but he decided to fly—because it was exciting! Ordinarily he did not have a reason or the money to fly anywhere. But he loved to take the family on a Sunday drive that would take them past the Troutdale airport where we'd look at the planes. No doubt he had fantasies of owning a plane—or even riding in some of them. He would have made a good pilot, and he looked the part: thin mustache, black hair slicked back, an easy grin.

Albert Howard and Hildah Drake in 1940, about to go riding on their 1930s Harley-Davidson.

All during the 1940s he owned motorcycles. It seemed to me that he usually got them by trading—a car, a pocket watch, some cash. After he got the first one he traded it for another, hopefully better machine. So far as I know the cycles were all American built, mostly Harley-Davidson, maybe an Indian. On Saturday morning he'd fire up his motorcycle, the noise reverberating off the garage and house, a thin blue smoke rising above the trees, and when the motor was warmed he'd put me on that big gas tank, my feet dangling into exhaust heat. He'd put the hand shift in low and ease the motorcycle into the road; when he was rolling he'd put one hand around me, the other working the gas. Ahead were two gas caps, a big speedometer and the road unfolding. I may have been apprehensive but never fearful, because I trusted my father to keep us safe.

My mother was less certain. I have a photo of my mother and father going cycle riding. My father looks relaxed while my mother looks apprehensive. I still have her jodhpurs and cycle boots, and they do not show any wear, so I don't think she went riding often. My father, on the other hand, went riding whenever he could. He did not belong to a club, but he knew a bunch of guys who had cycles and whenever he could get away from home he'd ride with them up the Columbia Gorge or around Mt. Hood. I envision the bunch stopping at a funky old tavern on a rural road for refreshments. My father did not drink much, but he always had beer in the refrigerator. He loved to smoke, store-bought when possible or he'd roll his own. What a way to spend a day: drinking an Oly, smoking a couple of butts, hanging out with his buddies and then roaring down the open highway on two wheels.

Meanwhile, my mother was at home, certain that he'd been in a wreck, worried sick, wringing her hands, wondering how she'd raise two kids by herself! Of course, she had something to worry about: motorcycles were dangerous! But the only accident my father had on a cycle was late one night coming home from work in the shipyard. He was riding home with a couple other guys on cycles and there was an intersection where a cop would wait for them. They tried to outrun him and my father was doing okay until he hit a pair of streetcar tracks and his cycle went down. He came home with cuts and bruises on his hands and a bad cut over one eye. He never said whether the cop caught him.

It was in this context that I knew I wanted a motorcycle. When I was eight I got a bicycle, and within a few months, as soon as my legs got long enough, I began to ride it around the neighborhood in a reckless manner. I would zoom around corners and speed down hills. In the athletic area behind Lents grade school I would put the bike into a long slide in the fine gravel. When I was twelve I began riding my bicycle on the motorcycle trails at an old stone quarry called Indian Rock; this was fairly dangerous at times because a cycle has a compression release or a kill button to slow it down but there was no way to slow a bicycle down on some hills, especially if the ground happened to be muddy. I dreamed of mounting an engine on that bike so that I could coast forever, without effort. When I got a paper route I dreamed of getting something motorized, like a Whizzer, or a Doodlebug, or a Cushman scooter, but my father pointed out that I needed a driver's license and insurance to ride those things, and I was too young.

I just had to wait.

Al Drake's 1947 BSA twin (and in the background his 1947 Ford mild custom).

My First Motorcycle

The first of anything is a big deal, and that's certainly the way I felt about my first motorcycle. The interesting thing about it as I look back is that it didn't kill me.

In high school I owned several cars, but I didn't get a motorcycle until 1954, when I was 19. I worked at Frank Costanzo Automotive, a garage/speed shop, and two blocks away, at 20th and N.E. Sandy, there was a small used car lot on a pie-shaped piece of land. I never gave the place special attention until one day, parked in the middle of the lot, were about twenty motorcycles. That day I walked to the lot on my lunch hour and checked out the bikes. They were mostly British bikes, but there was one from Italy that was rare and interesting: a Moto-Guzzi Falcone with a single horizontal cylinder, an outside flywheel, and a kick-starter on the left, the only motorcycle I've ever seen with that design. I can't remember the price, it probably wasn't much, but that bike interested me as a curiosity. I was much more interested in the British bikes, the Triumphs, the BSAs, Matchless and AJS. I loved the look of their tanks, aluminum engines, chrome handlebars and neat seats. I'd been reading *Cycle* for years, and I knew something about these bikes. I also knew that one could buy hop up kits, with tuned megaphone pipes, for not too much.

I can't remember how many times I walked to the lot, just to look. Nor can I remember individual bikes. Nor can I remember the owner's name, although I've asked numerous people who should of known; I think it was Archie Stanley, a Portland car dealer, who was a prime mover in buying land in Clackamas, just south of Portland, and building a TT track known as the Sidewinders track. It was a big deal for over thirty years, with some outstanding racers competing there, and when it was sold the owners came away with a big chunk of money.

I'd like to say that I went to that lot enough times to find the best motorcycle, but I probably found the worst one. It was a 1947 BSA 30.50 twin, with battered exhaust pipes and a dented tank. On the other hand, it had good tires and seats. And it ran! I must have lain awake nights thinking about this cycle, because one day I walked to the lot with $200 in my coveralls pocket and bought it. This purchase was a big deal! I earned only a buck an hour, which meant I had to work about six weeks to make the purchase. Moreover, I have never learned to dicker; looking back I think that bike was worth about $50. It was seven years old and worn out.

But at the time it was pure excitement. The owner asked whether I knew how to ride and I said no. He pushed the cycle out of the lot and onto the sidewalk, and then started it. He told me to get on, told me to engage the clutch, then kicked the shift level into low. This is the gas, he said, pointing at the right hand grip, give it some gas, let the clutch out and you're on your way. He probably told me where the front and rear brake controls were, and that I would have to kick the shift lever down to get into a higher gear, but the lesson seemed to consist of only a couple sentences. There was no big parking lot where I could practice working the controls. He gave me a slap on the back, and, like a scared horse, I was off. I drove down the street for a block, and, still in low gear, I pulled in the clutch and made a sharp right hand turn, heading back to the garage; the cycle jerked a couple times and stopped. I kicked the kick starter several times without luck; it felt as though the motor had no compression. I felt helpless. I'd ridden it only a block, hadn't even got out of low gear, and already I'd broken something—maybe the clutch, maybe even the crankshaft. Dismayed, I pushed the cycle back to work, where I leaned it against the wall of the garage (among the things it lacked was a kickstand). All afternoon I was in a funk, trying to think what I should do.

A few minutes before five I went out and tried to start the bike, but now I had the sense to put the shift lever in neutral; on the second kick it roared to life. Earlier I had not broken anything, I had disengaged the clutch and kicked the starter with the engine in gear–an easy mistake for a guy who had never ridden a cycle. I decided to leave the cycle at work and drive my car home. I don't think I was afraid to ride the cycle; in fact, I was excited to get on it, but I was cautious.

The next day I pushed the cycle back out on the sidewalk and thought about it all morning. At noon I wolfed down a sandwich and got on the cycle; it started right away. I carefully thought about the controls, then slowly moved onto a side street. I went fast enough to shift into second and I slowly went around corners. I wanted to drive down Sandy, a four-lane street, but I was again cautious. I worried about cars, but I also worried about getting back to work before my lunch hour was over.

That evening I waited until 5:30, when most of the rush hour traffic had passed, before attempting to ride the cycle home. It was a real thrill to be moving down the street, to shift from low to second to third, to crank the throttle and feel the cycle respond. I took it easy as I rode east on Glisan until I came to 82nd, a main road; there was traffic, but no one seemed to mind a kid on a motorcycle putting along at 35 mph. Every mile I rode I gained confidence, that I had mastered a strange machine, and that the movement of the controls was almost becoming natural. That, I have read, is when most people have an accident on a motorcycle, when they think they know what they're doing, but have not gained enough experience to know how to handle the cycle when they get in a jam. I stopped for a light at Division, and when it changed I went through the gears, then started down the hill towards Powell. I kept the throttle open until I was flying, the wind blurring vision, blowing my hair back in lines of speed, my dirty coveralls flapping against me. I loved the sound of the bike's exhaust and the sense of speed. I was caught up in the mystique of motorcycling, but I'm sure I would not have been able to handle the bike if someone had pulled in front of me or stopped quickly. I don't like to think what would have happened, but at the time such a disaster had not occurred to me.

Two things saved me until I got more experience. One, there was far less traffic then than there is today, and two, the bike lacked an instant response; it was mushy and while it would go 70 mph, it took a while to get there. It was worn out. I rode it around for a while, then decided to do a valve job. I knew nothing about motorcycle engines, but to my credit I was not afraid to take this one apart. I pulled the tank, then the head and finally the barrels. I took the head to work and ground the valves. When I miked the barrels my suspicions were confirmed: one piston must have broken and scored the walls badly enough to have it sleeved. One cylinder was about .050" smaller than the other. I got a set of new rings which fit one cylinder perfectly; the other rings I filed by hand until they fit the smaller hole. When I got everything together the motor ran, and a little better than before. I painted the tank yellow with a black scallop, but I did not fix the dent.

    Other than that I rode the bike a lot, but I must not have trusted it because I never went far from home. About a mile from my home was an old stone quarry, called Indian Rock. It was intersected with trails and had a couple steep climbs cut by cycles. I loved to go there in any kind of weather and rip around. The cycle still lacked instant response, and I think that kept me out of trouble. My friend Bob Kaseweter got a 1951 BSA single and we began riding together.

Al Drake on his 1951 BSA Gold Star. Alloy engine, big carb. Bike was like new.

My First Motorcycle

He had two neighbors who had cycles, and they roughed out an egg-shaped track over two back yards; they had races there, and although I loved the noise and excitement my bike was mushy and slow, and it kept me out of trouble.

Six months later, in February, 1955, I traded the BSA twin and $200 cash for a beautiful 1951 BSA Gold Star; it was quick, and I could have easily got in trouble with it if I had not got a lot of necessary experience riding the twin. There is an Andrew Wyeth painting titled "Young America", showing a boy riding a fat tired Schwinn bike, two fox tails hanging from the handle grips. I think of that painting when I think of myself, long ago, young, full of life, speeding down that hill on 82nd Avenue, the wind tearing at my eyes, blowing my hair back, my dirty coveralls flapping wildly.

Al "Bud" Drake (left) and Bob Kaseweter on their BSAs.

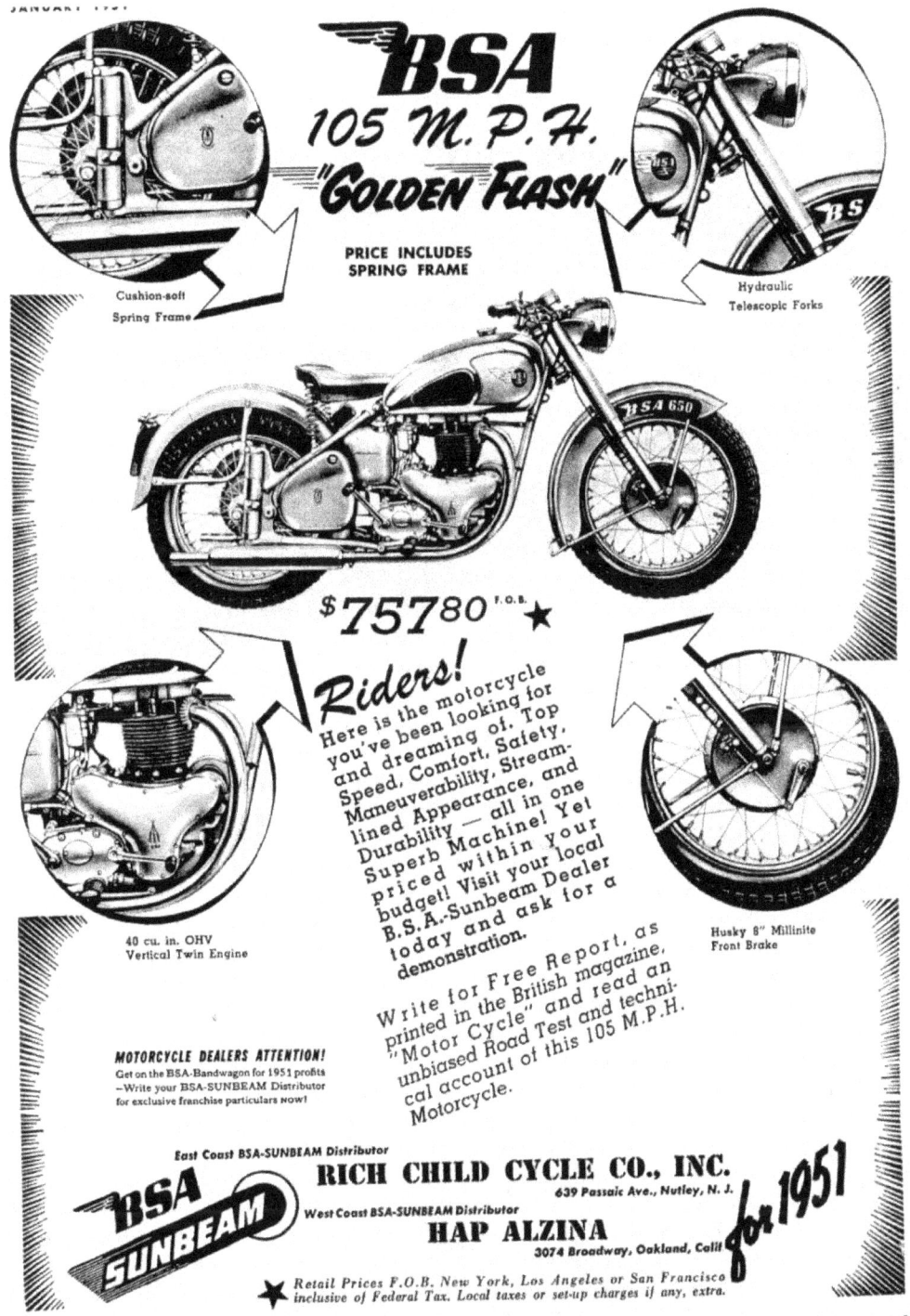

Johnny Payne with his '39 Pontiac taking his motorcycle to the race track.

Johnny Payne

Of course, there were motorcycles in Portland before I was aware of them. In fact, the area has a rich history. I was reminded of that one day when I was talking with Johnny Payne, an old biker.

"In the beginning, in the 1930s, I belonged to the Portland American Motorcycle Association (AMA) club, which was all Indians. Roy Burke belonged to it, Red Rice, Blackie Blackburn, Shadow Johnson, others. We were an all-Indian group, and the Rose City Motorcycle Club was an all-Harley group, and the Flying 15 was half-ass everything. But I didn't join the Flying 15 until I started my motorcycle business. Rocky Ryan belonged to it, and John Lockwood and Tattersall. Tattersall also worked for me for a while.

"I had a Crocker short tracker which I raced at Jantzen Beach. Victor Ascenzi rode it and so did Harry Nelson. Harry wouldn't turn the throttle on and Victor didn't like the way it handled. Red Rice used to ride it down in California and he went like hell with it. Jantzen Beach track was the same size as they raced short trackers on—the Class A machines. They were mostly all JAPs and my Crocker and a couple British machines. The British machines weren't very fast, and they weren't very good either. The JAPs went the best.

"I also raced at the old race track in Oregon City. I had a Harley Peashooter factory machine. It was a Harley-Davidson, single cylinder, 21 cubic inches, with no transmission and no brakes. It was like a CA Harley but the CA was a 30.50. Ansenberger had a CA Harley that he ran at Jantzen Beach. He rode it real well but some of the machines didn't have enough steam. He bought it from Charlie Ferrier who used to ride it at Oregon City. Charlie bought it down in California. It was made by Harley but it'd go like a JAP. That was before the war (WW II).

"The Oregon City track was the old fairgrounds track. It was an old dirt track, maybe a little longer than a half mile. I was going around practicing on my Harley one Saturday and the damn throttle stuck! I was going down the back stretch and I knew I had to shut it off to get around the corner, if I didn't I'd end up in the god damn grandstands. So I got off of it. That was the best thing I could think of. I just stepped off and rolled into a tight ball. I was probably going 70. I didn't get hurt because I rolled into a ball. Everybody came over and wondered what the hell happened. I said, well, I had to get off that thing. If I could've shut it off and then got back on the throttle I'd of been all right but I wasn't able to do that. It had a compression release but it was clear out of the way and you had to lift it up with your foot. Besides, Charlie Ferrier was practicing with his machine, he was behind me, on the other side of the track. To be honest, I didn't think fast enough. I just said, let me off this thing.

"After that I didn't ride it anymore. I sold it to Pat Conolly. Pat had a bunch of 21" singles."

1947 Jantzen Beach racing program featuring Speedway Motorcycles.

1951 Catalina Grand National

Les Connor (right) and friend on their bikes in the late 1940's

The Oregonian, 1952

Merhar's Drive-In

Merhar's Drive-In was a favorite hangout for motorcycles. Located on SE 82md one block south of Foster, it was open 24 hours a day. Originally it had been a Triple-X, built in the shape of two huge barrels, but in the 1940s that building was torn down and a new one built. The Triple X had fronted on 82nd, while the new building sat at a right angle to that busy street. The parking lot was never paved, so that by the early 1950s it had bumps and mud puddles, which discouraged the hot rodders who liked to keep their cars clean. They went to Flanagan's Drive-In at SE 82nd and Powell. Across the street directly south of Merhar's was XL Doughnuts, a small building built probably in the 1930s; it had the best doughnuts in town. The building is still there. To the east, across 82nd, was Chinese Alley, a good restaurant with a busy bar.

One of the bikers who spent a lot of time in Merhar's was Bill Langley. He recently recalled, "John and Hank Merhar owned it, two brothers. It was a rough place, with lots of fights, broken windows. All the roughnecks, because that was the place for all the hooligans in town. Even I used to get in some brawls there on a Friday or Saturday night. Everybody hung out there.

"I met my first wife there. We used to go to Watkins Park, dance and booze it up, and then come back to Merhar's at one or two o'clock, and eat, or sit there and drink coffee, BS until three or four o'clock in the morning. You could go in Merhar's on a Friday night and have one helluva good time and only spend a couple dollars. Something going on in there all the time, from a fist fight to some guy riding through on his motorcycle. All the time. Oh, we had a lot of fun in those days.

"I knew all the bikers. My dad was a motorcycle cop. Before he was a cop he was a bike rider and everybody knew everybody. I knew Red Rice. His dad was Dawes and his stepmother was Bertha; they spanked my ass when I was a kid. I grew up on SE 74th between Clinton and Woodward, just off Division. I know just about everybody in this town who ever rode a motorcycle. I used to play on Indian Rock, on Mt. Scott, all those horse trails and rabbit trails up there years ago.

"Merhar's had a lot of characters. Speed Mulday, the Azars, Cliff Majhor. We had parking places at the end, near the door, and we put our names there, where we used to park our bikes. Bill LeBeck, he hung out there. He got killed on 82nd. He had just got a haircut and was crossing 82nd, jay-walking, and some guy in a car nailed him. There was one guy who hung out there, Bob Shugar, he didn't ride but everybody knew him. He got killed in his shop one Friday night. A bulldozer blade came down and trapped him. He laid there until Monday morning before someone found him.

"Then there was a guy, Clay Schultz—Cookie, we called him. He went into Merhar's one morning and pumped up his Coleman stove and started fixing breakfast! They threw his ass out of there! There were a bunch of dingalings that

Merhar's Drive-In

hung out there. The Dummy—Aboo—he was a deaf mute. Helluva good rider. He hung out with Cliff Majhor when he worked with Joey Chitwood.

"One night we was all sitting in Merhar's when a woman pulls in there in a car, stark naked, and walked through the room, went out the door, got in her car and drove off. Never said a word! Then there was a guy we called Odd Ball. John Merhar threw him out of there four or five times. The last time that happened Odd Ball backed his '34 Ford pickup up to the door and revved it up; that truck smoked so bad, it filled the room and you couldn't see the guy sitting across the table from you! Guys would ride their bikes from the parking lot into Merhar's. I rode through there a couple times. Cliff Majhor rode inside, cut a doughnut and rode out; the black circle was on the floor for months!

"There were some pretty tough cookies that hung around Merhar's, two of the toughest were the Truxell boys. One night they were at the Foster Gardens drinking beer and some guy ran in there trying to get away from the cops and the cops were slapping him around. They bumped Walt Truxell and he decked a cop. Then the cop's partner jumped in and Walt's brother jumped in and they beat the crap out of those cops. It was some time before they could show their faces in this area. They had a reputation as a couple guys you didn't want to mess with.

"It's different today. It isn't like it used to be."

Officers Subdue Motorist, File Additional Charges

A persistent traffic violator was chased into a S. E. Foster road drive-in by prowl officers early Saturday and forcibly removed to jail when he first broke and ran and then defied officers to take him from the restaurant.

Veryl D. Kinne, 21, 2835 S. E. 122d avenue, was first cited at S. E. 72d avenue and Foster road by Officers Earl S. Morehouse and Howard E. Wold, on a charge of violation of the basic rule by driving 42 miles per hour in a 25-mile zone. Kinne drove away at a high rate of speed after the citation was issued.

The officers gave chase and Kinne again disregarded the siren signaling him to a halt. Kinne, the officers reported, stopped at the entrance of Merhar's Drive-in, 5629 S. E. 82d avenue, where he was placed under arrest for the second time.

Soft Approach Fails

Instead of submitting to arrest, Kinne drove his car into the restaurant parking lot and defied officers to take him. They took him by the arm and asked him to come peacefully. Instead he broke away and ran into the drive-in.

There he refused to come and notified officers they would have to remove him forcibly. That proved to be a 15-minute struggle which ended with the handcuffs on Kinne and his head cut by the glass from a swinging door.

A near riot developed, officers reported, in the drive-in when two ringleaders attempted to incite the more than 20 people in the restaurant to take action in Kinne's behalf.

An additional booking of disorderly conduct by resisting arrest was made against Kinne at the station. Bail was set at $400. A records check disclosed Kinne had been arrested three times on charges of larceny from an automobile or a car trailer and numerous traffic and curfew violations.

The Oregonian, 10/23/1949

Who Rode

You saw us
even the smallest
the most innocent
struck fear/ anger
in your heart

arrogant/ loud
we smelled frankly
of oil/ gas/ leather
of death

the distant scruump
of our exhaust suggested death
on a dished-out track
on a back road
a parted chain
split tank
the rider popping in flames

and you gathered together
your daughters

arrogant on corners/ bikes on jiffy stands leaned
to their shadows like question marks/ all in a row
arrogant on corners we stood/ tattoos/ side-burns/ dirty
long hair greased to a duck's ass/ broken teeth/ grinning
like death heads/ cig pack rolled in the T-shirt sleeve

we were everything the journalists promised/ mad/ dirty
geared to speed/ noise/ the joys of jagged exhaust
riding the devil's own hell on wheels/ cutting wheelies
speeding on public streets at night without lights
no respect for private citizens/ traffic/ laws/ cops
heading toward our hard uncertain destiny
we'd never heard of crash helmets/ skid lids

girls loved us
their narrow thighs
cased in tight levis
breasts hard
against riveted jackets
kidney belts were girdles
lips red enameled

they rode
the pillion
scarfs fluttering
arms around the rider
tight
holding on for life

and off the pavement
a quiet meadow
a cold beer
lying on leather
cooling fins clicking away all heat

Allan Tessman ran his Triumph at the drags. From left, Frank Tucker, Allan Tessman, Bill Killen, Jim Flittens and a fifth unidentified rider.

Cliff Majhor on his Matchless single. (Langlitz Collection)

Cliff Majhor

I lived at 97th and Duke in 1942, then I went in the service. Most of the cycle trails on Mt. Scott were made by the Clay Brothers, and most of them were made on Harleys. They'd take the front cylinder off and just run one cylinder, so they weighed less and they had more traction. When they put two cylinders on they didn't go faster, they just had a little more muscle so they could pull a sidecar. They'd put chains on the back wheel, like hill climbers, and that'd bull all the roots out, made some smooth trails. That'd be Roy Clay, Frank Clay, Rudy Young and Doc Lehman. I lived on Mt. Scott before I lived on Duke Street. I lived at the edge of Clackamas County, just before you go down the hill. I was supposed to go to Milwaukie high, but I was working in a ship yard, at Commercial Iron works, just below the Ross Island Bridge, and I worked graveyard shift and I didn't want to go clear out to Milwaukie. So I had to pay my own tuition to go to Franklin High, because I was out of the county. I worked graveyard shift, and went to school during the daytime.

I had my motorcycle all the time. I started riding a motorcycle when I lived in Scappoose, when I was a sophomore in high school, I was 14. The guy who taught me how to ride was Emil Kreofsky, we just buried him yesterday. He taught me how to ride in 1939. I lived on Mt. Scott, riding trails. I had an American bike, a Harley first, then an Indian, but I couldn't go on those trails, didn't have enough ground clearance, it'd hang up so I'd ride part-way up, turn around and come back. But after the war I bought an English bike, I got me a Matchless, then I could go on those trails. I made a lot of the trails myself, after 1948. Roy Clay used to have the gas station at 82nd and Johnson Creek Boulevard, he was there for years. Roy Clay's Shell station. Roy just died a year or two ago—he was past 90. They'd take one cylinder off, put skid chains on the rear tire and go up and down those hills. That chain would pull all the roots out so nothing ever grew there again. I'll bet If you went up there now all those trails are still there.

I rode at Indian Rock all the time—I made lots of the trails there. I made a lot of trails, feet up, where you couldn't put your feet down. Round, and up over the humps, tight turns, and at the back there was a square up there and you had to go fast and ride over on the rear wheel or you couldn't make it. Go across that creek, we had a little bridge there and come up that hill. We'd make a tough hill and then guys would go up there with a shovel and make it easy and ruin it! Us older guys, we like the tough shit, right? But the kids wanted to make it up the hill so they'd go home and get a shovel and come back and dig the trails so anybody could ride over them.

Finally somebody got hurt at Indian Rock and the parents tried to sue Dwyer's, so they kicked us out of there for good. Dwyer had the airfield below and of course the mill. They kicked our ass out in the middle 1950s.

Cliff Majhor

After the war I lived at 78th and Flavel, and I lived there until about 1948. When they subdivided they named a street after us, there's a Majhor street between Flavel and Malden—Majhor Court.

I started hanging out at Merhar's Drive in in 1941, and I spent a lot of time there. It was still the Triple-X then. They put the new building in after the war, about 1946 (or 1947). That double-decker hamburger they had—I used to come in there and I didn't want two hamburgers, but I wanted more meat. In those days, hamburger buns weren't cut, you had to cut them yourself. We made a 2 by 4 for Neva Litcher, the cook, with two cuts in it, and she'd put a bun on that board and make two cuts, then she'd put two pieces of meat on the bun. We started making double-deckers there in 1941, and McDonald's didn't start until 1959. If you find an old Merhar's menu, you'll see a Majhor Special listed. Guys I knew would come here from all over, and we'd eat at Merhar's and they'd say "Lookee here, this guy's got his own sandwich on the menu!"

We all hung around Merhar's. Sometimes you'd go there and there'd be twenty motorcycles parked in front. But none of us were drinkers, so old John and Hank, they liked us, because we didn't cause any problems. We were all just sandwich eaters and coffee drinkers, and they liked having us around there. I went in through the swinging doors one time on my cycle and burned a circle on the floor, cut a doughnut. Boy, that black mark was there for years. It would've come off with a little scrubbing, but he was proud of that. I went through the double doors, burned that circle and went right back out again. That was really neat! My signature was right inside the door. Guys say, "The Fonz was nothing," the shit they used to do back then. Those guys knew how to kick the juke box and get it playing without putting in money, and how to kick the pinball machine and get a free play, those guys knew all that shit.

I practically lived at Merhar's. It was open 24 hours a day, seven days a week. You could sit back in the corner, not bothering nothing, they'd come back and kick you once in a while to wake you up if you were sleeping. The owners of Merhar's, John and Frank are dead, but Hank is still alive. We went to John's birthday party a few years ago and Hank was there, and he was so glad to see all of us. It brought a tear to his eye. They came here, to Portland, out of Montana, about 1939, and started Merhar's. Those were some damn good times.

Bob Tiesley, Buge, Hilger, all the Mt. Scott guys hung out there. They'd drink at the Checkered Flag, at 82nd and Flavel, but they'd come to Merhar's to eat. That club still meets every month, has a club house up on the bluff near Meadows Tavern on Johnson Creek Boulevard. Lots of old photos on the walls. Frank Clay, he had a photography studio, and he sold photographs. Lots of photos of Mt. Scott in the late 1930's, when they first started making the trails there. That club started in 1940 at the Bob White Theater—actually, it was right next to the theater, at the Punjab Tavern.

John Anton—he was a dance instructor at Arthur Murray Dance Studio. Got a bad eye, so he was kind of cross-eyed. And to make extra money he flagged wide loads, from Tucson to Canada, stuff like that on his motorcycle. Remember old Slim Jim, big tall guy—you'd ask him how tall he was and he'd say 5' 18" – He was 6' 6". Al Lowrey, he had A-1 Electric, and he rode a Maico. About 82nd and Holgate.

We used to have coasting races down Mt. Scott—clear from the top of the hill, on Mt. Scott Blvd, coast around the cemetery, clear down past Johnson Creek Boulevard. Dead engine from the Clackamas county line. If you were chickenshit you'd put the brakes on and you couldn't coast that far. Sometimes we'd have ten guys line up for a race.

Then we'd go up 112th and ride down—it's so steep you couldn't see the pavement ahead. Doc Lehman had a house up there, right on a curve back in the woods. He had a race track built in yard and we'd go up there and race. I remember 112th was gravel, then they finally put some tarmac on it.

Cliff Majhor riding his cycle through a burning wall. (Langlitz Collection)

Officer's Cycle Injures Boy, 8

James Manny, 8, of 6112 Southeast Eighty-third avenue, suffered a probable skull fracture, a left leg fracture and back injuries Saturday when struck by the motorcycle of Special Officer Bob Dillon, 26, Gainsborough apartments, on Southeast Eighty-second avenue near Ramona street.

Dillon was on duty as a funeral escort at the time of the crash. Accident Investigator Frank Pratt Jr. said the boy apparently darted between the cars in the procession. Dillon was treated at emergency hospital for scalp lacerations, a sprained right shoulder and abrasions to both legs, right elbow and left wrist. The boy was taken to Portland sanitarium.

Dillon, a "daredevil" motorcycle artist, was featured in the recent police exhibition at Multnomah stadium when he drove his cycle through a burning wall.

The Oregonian, June, 1940

Special Notices

I WILL NOT be responsible for debts other than my own. Donald A. Newgent, 847 E Maple, Hillsboro, Or.
I WILL NOT be responsible for any debts other than my own. Ruth S Collins, 4407 SW Kelly.
PLEASE anyone who saw motorcycle spill nr. St. Vincent hospital about 2:30 pm May 6 contact Hoss, BR 2396.

PERSONAL MESSAGES

ETHEL—WRITE TO YOUR OLD PAL. WITH LOVE, ME.

Young Cyclist And Auto Crash

Reportedly thrown about 20 feet through the air after a motorcycle he was riding was struck by a machine driven by Patrolman Byron H. Shields at N. W. 2d avenue and Everett street, Jerome Cohen, 16, of 2216 S. W. 2d avenue, was taken to Good Samaritan hospital Tuesday for treatment of right side injuries.

According to police, Patrolman Shields was attempting to arrest the driver of a third vehicle, a "speeder" he had been following for some distance, at the time of the accident.

The Oregonian, July, 1940

Cycle Rider Skids

Anton B. Christianson, 22, of 4617 Southeast Harrison street, was in St. Vincent's hospital Sunday suffering a possible skull fracture and facial lacerations. He was injured, attendants were notified, when his automobile went into the ditch near Beaverton.

Lewis Sherman, 21, of 2029 Northwest Hoyt street, was taken to Portland sanitarium Sunday night after his motorcycle got out of control and skidded sidewise for 50 feet near Northeast Fiftieth avenue and Foster road.

He suffered a back injury, cuts and bruises. No other vehicle was involved in the accident, Traffic Investigator George Phillips said.

The Oregonian, March, 1940

Motorcycles

'48 HARLEY-DAVIDSON 3-wheel motorcycle delivery. Low mileage, good condition. LOEPER CHEVROLET CO., Baker, Or.

INDIANS, A J S MATCHLESS motorcycles. Cushman motor scooters, Schwinn-built bicycles. RAY E. GARNER, 1040 SE Morrison, EA 6444.

FULL LINE OF '52 TRIUMPHS AND ARIELS, $695 AND UP. WESTERN MOTORCYCLES 307 NE BROADWAY GA 2914

NEW BSA singles, twins, $595 up. Good clean used English-American mch. Terms. Allied M. C. Sales, 3706 SE Powell, VE 5406.

SELL OR TRADE new Triumph speed twin for cycle or sound projector. TA 6340.

1950 TRIUMPH Thunderbird, perfect cond. Reasonable. Trade equity on car. 1935 NW Raleigh.

1950 THUNDERBIRD. Top shape. $425. Terms. 3415 NE Hancock. MU 5455 or VE 7575.

'40 61 overhead Harley-Davidson motorcycle, $185, 1 new tire, fair cond. EV 1-7095.

MUST SELL Matchless 1949 motorcycle. Exc. buy for cash. KE 6682.

3-WHEEL delivery cycle. 1948. Gd. cond. New rubber, $165, terms. SU 3838.

'35 IND. Scout, new carb. Rblt. batt. Gd. tires. $75 cash as is. MU 4090.

1950—74HD, 4200 miles, lots of extras. UN 5607.

CUSHMAN motor scooter, excellent mechanical condition. $75. Ph. LI 6058.

1941 INDIAN 4-cyl. New o'haul. Lots of accessories. Gd. cond. $140. CH 4527.

1950 EXCELSIOR 197 CC, 2-cycle with bags. TA 2917.

1948 HARLEY 45, windshield, buddy seat, saddle bags. Good cond. EA 2834.

'41 HARLEY 61 OHD. All new parts. $230. MU 0050. 5018 NE Prescott.

CUSHMAN motor. Gd. cond. $125. TW 3941.

MOTOR SCOOTER for sale, reasonable. KE 1034.

'42 HARLEY-D. 45. Exc. running shape. $195. 2203 SW 5th.

The Oregonian, August, 1952

Al Drake riding the rear wheel at Indian Rock.

Where We Rode

Mostly we rode on public streets. Traffic was slower and lighter in those days, and streets were not congested. Oh, there was the 8:00 am and 5:00 pm rush hours, but traffic was nothing like it is today. Even stop lights were not a problem because there were far fewer lights. When cars were stopped at a light it was common for a cyclist to ride slowly between the two rows of car, moving to a place at the head of the line and then ripping off when the light changed to green.

With far fewer cars on the road the chances of a cyclist getting in a wreck were greatly reduced. Cars in the 1950s were not very fast. A good bike could accelerate faster than an Oldsmobile 88, the fastest car around. A biker owned the road, although, then as now, you hoped that some turkey in a car would not turn in front of you!

In those days there was a lot of vacant land that did not seem to belong to anyone, even in the city. There were footpaths that cut diagonally across fields, and trails worn smooth by pedestrians. These were perfect places on which to ride a cycle, and they were the places a guy would head if he were being chased by the police, especially at night.

HILL CLIMBS:

I went to several hill climbs with my father during the 1940s but today I'm not certain where some of them were. The location required an incredibly steep hill, one that would challenge the abilities of man and machine; the average rider could not ascend such hills. Even competitive riders, who had plenty of horsepower and chains wrapped around the rear tire for traction, had trouble. It was common to see a rider reach the three quarter point and as the hill grew steeper the rider would sense the hopelessness of the situation and step off his cycle, letting it crash end over end to the bottom of the hill. Sometimes a rider would stay on his machine a little too long and when the rear wheel really dug in the front wheel would lift and the cycle would go over backwards.

There was a hill climb site at 158th and SE Powell, on a farm which was, or later became, a dairy. That was out in the country in those days.

Another site was somewhere in S.W. Portland, not far from downtown. It had a lot of parking space for spectators' cars and motorcycles, and a long, steep hill. Everything has changed so much in Portland it's hard for me to imagine where the site was located.

Another spot for hill climbing was on the side of Rocky Butte. Don Krueger remembers that place. "The hill climb started in the gravel pit off 82nd Avenue and ran up the west side of Rocky Butte. That got steep! You gotta have balls for that one!"

One of the best hill climb riders in the country was Roy Burke of Portland, Ore. Old timers still tell stories about his riding skills. Allegedly, he would load his specially-built hill climbing bike on his trailer and tow it to a major meet in Laconia, New Hampshire. He'd unload the bike, fire it up and ascend the hill in record time, then he'd head back to Portland. He'd make the 6,000 mile round trip in order to make the one minute run up the hill!

THE OLD HOMESTEAD:

Hare and Hound events were popular in the 1950s. A course was laid out beforehand, and, if possible, it involved water, mud and brush. Riders raced around the course, and after a few laps the mud was really churned up; mud covered both men and machines!

There was an area in S.W. Portland known as The Old Homestead—it might have been the same place where that major hill climb was held. However, the terrain seemed different; the hill climb involved a large meadow while The Homestead involved a thick forest. I was at The Homestead only when an event was scheduled, and I do not know whether it was open at other times.

The Old Homestead (Takanori Okamoto Collection)

SWAN ISLAND:

Before they covered Swan Island with warehouses it was a large area of mud, sand and scrub brush. Motorcyclist had cut trails all through the brush and it was a good place to have a Hare and Hound event or simply to dice it up.

It was a long way from my house in southeast Portland to Swan Island and the times I went there was with a bunch of other bikers. We'd meet at Bart's Drive-In (later, The Speck) parking lot, at 50th and Powell, around 8:00 am

Sunday morning, a big bunch of us, guys from all over southeast Portland. We'd stand around, laugh, talk until someone decided it was time to leave. With our tanks full, we'd head west on Powell, maybe 50 singles and twins mixing it up .As a group we'd turn right on Union Avenue and head north. When we got to Killingsworth we'd turn left and head west until we got to St. Johns. In those days Portland was divided into many smaller neighborhoods, and for me St. Johns was another country; I never went there except for special occasions, such as the motorcycle run.

Most of the guys stopped at a small café on Killingsworth, to have breakfast or to let other bikers catch up. I'd stay on the sidewalk, partly because I never drank coffee and partly because I didn't have any money for breakfast. When we left the café, perhaps 200 cycles strong, we'd head west to St. Johns and then descend the hill until we got to the course.

INDIAN ROCK:

This was the place I knew best as it was only a short mile from my house and I spent lots of time there. To get there you drove east on Foster Road and turned right on S.E. 100th. You drove across the bridge over Johnson Creek and through Dwyer's mill. For about an eighth of a mile there were logs stacked fifty feet high beside the road, and beyond that was country. Almost immediately you drove up a rough road just wide enough for a car; the water that ran from above had cut deep ruts, and rarely would anyone attempt to drive a car up the road. In other words, the road was just right for a motorcycle. On both sides were small hills, the brush cut away by a generation of motorcycles. To the right was a steep but short rise with a narrow trail; above that was a plateau. To the left was a wide path that led uphill, then a few feet of level ground and then a steep rise to the top. Just about every rider could make it up to the first level but only the best riders could make it to the top. If you did get to the top you had to shut off immediately and swing to the right; if you built up too much speed you risked going over the other side, which was straight down.

If you continued on the main road you came to a large circular area. At the south side was a basalt cliff, and there were huge rocks everywhere. The place had been a quarry, but I never saw anyone remove dirt or rocks during the 1940s and 1950s. Before that, I was told, it had been a meeting place for Indians, but I never saw any Indians there. Beside the basalt cliff was a trail that seemed to go straight up; the tracks indicated that someone had ridden up it. All around to the west of the quarry area were trails.

It boggles the mind to realize that this rough area was a short distance from Foster Road. It was open to all, but usually there was no one there. I started playing on Indian Rock when I was a kid. If I had .50¢ I'd buy a box of shells and take my .22 rifle and pistol and shoot into the clay bank. Occasionally one or two others would use the place to go plinking with their guns. Many a night a friend and I would sleep up there. When I got older I rode my bicycle on the motorcycle trails, which was pretty hairy. Older yet I'd take a girl friend to Indian Rock and neck. In all the times I was there the place was generally empty, and even with the girls, guns and beer there was never any trouble.

Where We Rode

Indian Rock remained unchanged until, in the 1960s, the city mothers decided that it was a problem; the area was bulldozed, filled in and a road built over it. Only part of the east side remains the same; it's unsuitable for cycle riding.

Al Drake catching air. Rare shot of the big hill at Indian Rock–it was steep. All was leveled in the 1960s.

Riding Bike in the Fifties

Mort Becker and Ross Langlitz in front of the Peter Iredale.near Astoria, Oregon. (Langlitz Collection).

Gary Guthrie making a jump in 1960. Site is future I-205 freeway in Southeast Portland.

Sensations

riding in the rain
racing into a sheet of needles
no front fender the wheel throws
a wave at 20 mph/ a flood at 50

standing around the bike shop
talking/ talking for hours/ talking
of gears/ cams/ mags/ carbs/ girls/
black coffee/ cigarets/ the exhaust
of talk rising into honey-dark grease

skidding/ a hum/ panic
out of control/ the fear
knowing you're going to crash
try to lay it down/ slide/ horizon
tilting/ get your leg out from under
then slowly/ like a dream
sliding across pavement toward a curb
a tree/ a bumper/ sliding/ sliding

riding with the pack
thirty motors headed out/ sixty wheels
spinning in sun/ aluminum barrels
gear cases polished like jewels
most of all the pitched jagged exhausts
twins and singles mixing it up until
you can't hear what gear you're in

riding all day/ a line of mud
up your back/ mud three inches deep
on boots/ mud in the mouth
at dusk a cup of hot bitter coffee

from the bottom the hill climb
is impossible/ straight up
crack it/ pop clutch/ crank it on
full bore/ all the way in low gear
banking/ steeper/ engine rising
and falling/ wheel digging
feet on rear pegs/ lifting/ weight ahead
hold the bars down/ halfway
front wheel begins to lift/ forks extend
rear wheel digs/ front lifts/ coming up

Riding Bike in the Fifties

floats until you're looking over the tach
at blue sky/ falling backwards

Monday morning/ the ache of muscles
stretched and broken/ after a weekend
of riding trail/ climbing/lifting
300 pounds of bike through mud
over rocks/ beyond brush/ to impossible
heights/ and then getting it down

the bike shop walls are plastered
with old photos/ racers and riders
they grin in baggy clothes
a bottle of beer in each upraised hand
their women wear rosey the riveter slacks
flat track racers/ outlaw riders
board track racers/ hillclimb champions
where are they now?
dead on a dished-out track
a dished-out bed/ or selling spark plugs

I look in the photos for my father
he would be on a pre-war Indian/ Harley
black jodhpurs/ high boots/ white cap
I recall the war/ he worked
in shipyards/ Swan Island/ Oregon yard
he had only a B ration sticker
rode to the swing shift to save gas
he said they raced a cop every night
thundering through war-time streets
hand shift/ topped by a marble knob
suicide clutch/ fender fairings
one morning he came home his hand
cut open/ legs scraped/ bleeding
to miss a streetcar on wet tracks
he laid her down
and walked away from that one

Mort Becker and Ross Langlitz (Langlitz Collection)

Chaos

A recent obituary said that Mort Becker had died, and although it didn't mention that he had owned a motorcycle shop in the 1950s everything else indicated that this was the same guy I'd done business with.

Mort's shop was so obscure I don't think it had a sign, maybe not even a name. (I later learned it was called Modern Motorcycles.) But it was in an interesting neighborhood, with lots of automotive parts dealers around the point where Foster, Powell, and S.E. 50th intersect. Across Foster was Barker's Auto Supply, a general automotive store which was a major dealer for Porter mufflers, dual exhaust systems and speed equipment. Across Powell was The Speck Drive-in, a hangout for rodders. Next door to Mort's shop was the Creston Tavern, which by 1957 had become The Pink Bucket, Portland's first cool tavern. The building was painted black, inside and out, even the windows, with pink trim and a bunch of travel posters on the walls. Thanks to a new city law it had become possible to buy beer by the pitcher, and you could walk around with a cold beer; both illegal previously. That meant you could drink a lot more, and mingle while you were drinking.

Mort's shop should have been painted black. It was dark and dirty, with grease everywhere. As you entered there were two rows of used motorcycles for sale; on the other side of a low wall was the repair area, with a parts department at the rear. Most of the machines were oily, scuffed, dented. Some of them are more interesting today than they were then. The wooden floor absorbed grease, and cycle parts were everywhere. All that sounds negative, but it was what drew me to the place, the chaos of machinery, the sense of speed.

This was the kind of place that Steve McQueen would've hung around, if it'd been in California. He could've parked his Ferrari at The Speck, walked across the street to the tavern for a beer, then wandered into Mort's shop to see how work on his Crocker was proceeding. Except I'm sure that Mort's shop never had a Crocker under its roof. On the other hand, it did have a used WW II Harley for sale, with horizontal opposed cylinders, like a BMW, and a shaft drive, the only one I ever saw.

Most of the bikes were British—Triumph, BSA, Matchless, AJS, Ariel. These were the bikes that were the opposites of the big Harley-Davidsons. They were ridden by young guys, lean and hard, who stripped off whatever they didn't need and ran them both on and off road. A group of motorcyclists from the Sidewinders club got together and bought a few acres in Clackamas, south of Portland, and laid out a race track. It was a big deal, with lots of competition and crowds of spectators. Others competed, or at least diced it up, at the trials course laid out at Swan Island. Today Swan Island is covered with warehouses, but in the 1950s it was covered with brush and small trees, intersected with a maze of cycle trails.

I hung around Mort's shop because it was more casual than some other shops, such as Allied Cycle or East Side Cycle, where you felt pressured to buy a new cycle. Also, a couple guys I'd gone to high school with began working for Mort. Gene Curry, barely twenty, became a cycle mechanic, then a respected tuner and racer, who was offered a national number. So was John Farlow. When John rode with me and my friend, Bob Kaseweter, he had a 19" Velocette bored to 21"; it had pneumatic front forks, which were fully inflated in the morning but were bottoming out by noon. Bob and I called him "Sleepy John" but by the time he was offered a national number he was known as "Sliding John"!

Some Saturday mornings, Bob and I would ride to Mort's shop just to have a place to go; we had to ride somewhere. Or we'd race around Indian Rock, an old stone quarry with cycle trails near my house, and then we'd hang around Mort's. There were always racers or would-be racers to shoot the breeze with. One Saturday morning an old man came in and asked whether we wanted some old motorcycle parts. Kaseweter and I rode out to his farm, which was in Gresham, and found the pile of rusty parts half-covered with high grass. I don't think the old guy wanted money, but Bob and I decided to pass. I've often thought of that pile of junk, frames and forks and cylinders, which might have contained parts for an ancient Indian or Henderson.

I liked the idea of a modified cycle, with the fenders removed and a small gas tank in place of the stock one. There were plenty of bikes like that at Mort's, singles with polished alloy cases and barrel, a Triumph twin with megaphones. The shop did a good business putting swinging arm suspensions on the older rigid frame models by cutting the frame apart, building brackets and mounting a pair of automotive tube shocks on the back. Such a conversion helped the ride whether on or off pavement, especially if you rode a Triumph with a heavy spring hub.

I last saw Mort Becker at a banquet for old motorcycle guys. I wouldn't have recognized him, but he wore a large name tag. I introduced myself, but it was clear that he didn't remember me. I said, "I'm the guy who installed the push rods backwards on a BSA twin!" He thought, then said sure. Some forty years had passed, and if he did remember me it meant that I was the only guy dumb enough to have made such a mistake.

I bought my first motorcycle in August, 1954, and I got it off a used car lot that had bought a bunch of cycles. I paid $200, which I think was $150 too much. I worked in a garage for a buck an hour, which meant I worked for than 200 hours to pay for that cycle. It was a 1947 BSA 30.50 twin, kind of beat up, and lacking a front fender and a kickstand, which meant I always had to lean it against something. But those were cosmetics; it seemed to me that it didn't run right.

I wanted to improve the cycle, so I painted the blue gas tank yellow with black scallops (without removing the dent). I rode the cycle on the street (without insurance) and on trails. In retrospect, the cycle's main virtue was a controllable power. It was fast enough, but if it'd been really fast I would've been in trouble since I only thought I knew how to ride. I wanted more power so I tore the engine apart, even though I lacked a shop manual. The first thing I noticed was that one cylinder had been sleeved and that the piston was .050" smaller. I bought a set of rings, and filed the ends of the rings for the smaller piston. I took the head to work, where I did a valve job. When I got everything home I began to assemble the engine; I got everything back together and the last thing to do was to put the valve covers on. But they wouldn't fit.

Finally, I got my friend, Bob Kaseweter, to tow the bike to Mort Becker's shop. Bob had a pretty ugly '37 Ford sedan made into sort of a pickup. I don't know why we didn't put the cycle on the '37, but we tied a sturdy rope to the pickup, and the other end to the cycle's front fork. It required some skill to keep the cycle steady and the rope taut in Saturday traffic. Because the rope wasn't straight, the cycle wanted to pull to the right, but Bob took it easy and we were doing okay. It was a distance of less than three miles, and we were about halfway when a light rain began to fall. Then it rained harder. I had no front fender, and I'd removed the gas tank, so the water kicked up by the front tire hit me right in the face. Bob held his speed to about 25 mph but the wave of water hitting me felt like we were going a lot faster. I couldn't see a thing. I couldn't remove my hand from the handlebar because I was afraid the cycle would veer. I couldn't even shout to Bob because of the amount of water going into my mouth when I opened it. Somehow I was able to keep the rope taut and the cycle straight. My hair was soaked; water flew up into my eyes and dripped down into them. I felt dizzy, unsure what was up, what down, which direction was straight ahead. I was helpless, and submitted to the utter disorder and confusion.

Somehow we arrived. Then or later I thought: how could I be smart enough to dismantle an unknown engine and dumb enough to almost die in a deluge? Mort saw at a glance the problem: "The longer rods go in the front!" That was something I wrote on the wall of my garage in white chalk, and it's still there.

SAVE up to 85% IN WAR SURPLUS

AVIATORS' (AN-6530) WINDPROOF & DUSTPROOF GOGGLES
Chamois lined, rubber covered frames. Interchangeable, GROUND LENSES in clear or green. Has non-fogging breathers in frame. Adj. nose bar. Ideal for flying, cycling etc. NEW $3.95 USED $2.75

B-8 — ARMY AIR CORP GOGGLES — All rubber frame with inside chamois lining. Clear, shatter resistant lense. Comes with 7 interchangeable lenses, 2 amber, 4 green and 1 clear. $3.69

GENUINE ARMY AIR FORCE SUNGLASSES
6 Base. Finest quality, glare-free colator lenses, optically ground & polished. Gold plated frame is adjustable. Has Pearlized sweat bar and nose pads, cable temples. Beautiful leather case can be attached to your belt. HERE'S THE REAL McCOY $4.75

AIR FORCE TYPE SUNGLASSES
SG-4G — AIR FORCE Type GLASSES — 4 base, ground & polished processed glass lenses. Gold plated frame with Pearlized sweat bar and nose pads. Cable ear pieces, simulated leather case. $1.95

FLYING HELMETS
Summer type, lightweight canvas-rubber ear pads with soft Chamois interlining for radio receiver. With chin strap. NEW 69¢

455 - FLYING HELMET — Fine grade leather chamois lined with chin cup on strap. Intermediate weight for summer wear. ONLY $1.59

GENUINE LEATHER MOTORCYCLE JACKETS
Complete jacket made of Top Grade front quarter horsehide, zipper opening on sleeve at wrist and three zipper pockets. One built-in snap pocket. Snaps on collar and shoulders too. Has waist belt with large buckle. Form fitting waist and action back. Full lgth. zipper closure. Rich black color. Two styles - lined with rayon. Sizes 36-46. Rayon lined/leather collar $27.95 $32.50
Snap-on fur collar

230 Pg. CATALOG Packed with SENSATIONAL VALUES in WAR SURPLUS, FACTORY CLOSE-OUTS and GENERAL MERCHANDISE! 1000's of items for the Mfgr. Mechanic, Sportsman, Photographer, Hobbyist, Home Owner, etc. BIG SAVINGS on Clothing, Housewares, Hardware, Foam Rubber, Hand & Power Tools, Outdoor & Camp Equipment, and Gadgets. ILLUSTRATED Send Only 50¢ (for handling & mailing)

Prices are F.O.B. Los Angeles. Pay by M.O. or Check. 1/2 Deposit with C.O.D.'s.

PALLEY SUPPLY CO 2263 E. VERNON AVE. Dept. CV-7 LOS ANGELES 58, CALIF.

the "CASCADE"..

Our newest jacket, the "Cascade," is designed for mild weather riding and combines the good looks and wearing qualities available only in custom made leathers. The "Cascade" is built for action, for comfort . . . useful on or off your motorcycle. There's a trim two inch collar band, nothing to flap when riding without a windshield. No need to carry a heavy military style belt around and easy to pack when traveling . . . comfortable when sitting in a car. The "Cascade" comes with two large zippered pockets, heavy duty front zipper, zip sleeves. There's a generous lap-over back design to insure no gap between jacket and jeans and of course, our exclusive waterproof rayon twill lining and custom tailoring to your measurements. Price, postpaid, $37.50.

Before buying any jacket, slacks or breeches you owe it to yourself to get acquainted with Langlitz Leathers. Write today for our 1952 catalog, the most complete line of motorcycle clothing ever designed for the American rider. Langlitz Leathers are priced for all riders, yet custom made for each rider.

Langlitz Leathers
633 S.E. MORRISON ST.
PORTLAND 14, OREGON

AMERICA'S NEWEST LIGHTWEIGHT!

AMBASSADOR MOTORCYCLE

Equipped with the world famous 197 cc Villiers Engine. 90 miles per gallon. A lightweight with big machine performance.

$327 Retail Price
Including Federal Excise Tax
F.O.B. San Francisco

DEALERS INQUIRIES INVITED . . .

HAP JONES
235 VALENCIA ST.
SAN FRANCISCO 3-C,
CALIFORNIA
United States Distributor

Thoro Presents
THE SPEED SHIFT

Positive action

It's the berries for hare and hound English trials

Write for free literature

4-speed only, clutch works like 125 H.D.

INSTALL IN 1 HOUR

$42.50 plus tax
liberal discount to dealers

Post Office Box 166   North Aurora, Illinois

What We Wore

The biker's wardrobe was pretty simple: Levi's, T-shirt, leather jacket, boots, gloves and cap. That's what all bikers wore, and the clothing was practical as well as attractive, at least to bikers.

Levi's pants were cheap and tough; a pair cost about $3.00 in the 1950s. The snug-fitting tapered leg didn't catch on things and they didn't blouse out at speed. The material was tough, and a guy could ride through a blackberry patch without tearing the fabric. Levi's didn't show dirt or grease, and they could be worn for days without washing. There was a rumor that some guys wore Levi's until they would stand up by themselves!

A T-shirt was a T-shirt. They were cheap and plentiful. They were white, at least in the beginning, and I don't remember any T-shirts with advertising or writing on them. There may have been some club shirts, but I can't recall even one. I also don't recall anyone wearing a dress shirt or a flannel shirt, not even in cold weather. When you were riding off the road you worked up a sweat and a T-shirt was enough to keep you warm. Yes, they got dirty but you just tossed them in the dirty clothes pile and pulled on another one.

When I look at photos of bikers taken during the 1950s all the guys are wearing leather jackets. Some were made in Portland by Langlitz, some were made elsewhere, some came from Sears, Roebuck or another store and some were from WW II, the A-2 or G-1 flight jackets available for a few bucks at military surplus stores. Leather jackets were made to fit tightly, to hug the body, to cut the wind at speed, with just enough room under them for a T-shirt. They were warm without being hot. They were worn not because they were stylish but because they were tough and durable. If you were riding in the brush the jacket would absorb blows. If you fell off your cycle the jacket would save you from road rash.

Most bikers wore engineer boots; made of thick leather, with a belt across the top, they came about twelve inches up the leg. You could buy these boots at various stores and they were not expensive; Sears had them and they were priced at about $15.00 into the 1970s. Some guys would take them to a shoe maker and have a wedge inserted between the sole and the heel, so that the bottom of the boot was flat and couldn't catch on anything. All flat track racers wore such a boot, so the rider could put his left foot down when cornering. This might have been the origin of the term "hot shoe."

Mark Budlong remembers a different kind of boot that he wore in 1950. "They were British Navy boots, black, made of heavy leather, and they came up quite high, higher than an engineer boot, and they spread out at the top. There was this little (shoe repair) shop on southeast Foster Road, and the fellow there would narrow the top, so it didn't flute out, and he would put another sole on the bottom and make the bottom smooth, without an instep.

What We Wore

"That was what Don Tindall wore. He was my hero. Another thing the Tindall boys did, we thought they were the smoothest guys around, was to remove the leather patch on their Levi's."

Bob Knowles remembers a different kind of boot: "They were Linesman boots, such as telephone linesmen wore, that laced all the way up to the knee." Presumably they were worn with heavy boot socks.

A guy had to wear heavy boots because he was always banging his ankle on the pegs. And about half the time the kick starter would catch, then kick back and bang into your ankle or leg. Sometimes it hurt even with a heavy boot.

Hot rodders traditionally wore what is now called a "stroker" cap, the type of cap "Stroker McGurk" wore in Tom Medley cartoons. It was originally worn by butchers; it cost about a quarter, and was intended to be thrown away when it got dirty. Bikers wore a similar cap, but it was black and made of a heavier fabric and had a silk lining. The problem with these caps was that they would fly off at about 35 mph. Perhaps they would have worked better if they were worn backward, but I never saw anyone do that.

Ross Langlitz on his 1948 Velocette (Langlitz Collection)

A lot of guys wore gloves, at least in cold weather because they would keep your hands warm. I did not wear gloves most of the time. In cold weather I wore a pair of black leather gloves I bought from a friend. Then in 1955 I went deer hunting and nailed a big one; I traded the hide to the Thurlow Glove Company for a pair of gloves. They were light tan, fit tightly, and were so supple it felt like you were not wearing gloves. They were really deluxe dress gloves, and I should have not worn them riding bike because they soon got stained and greasy, but they fit wonderfully.

In 1954 I bought several items from a friend, Chuck Henry, who was the counterman at ABC Auto Supply. He decided to sell his cycle and get married and he figured he wouldn't need his riding togs anymore. For $20.00 I bought two leather jackets, one an early Langlitz and the other a Harley jacket, a pair of cycle boots with a wedge in the instep, a pair of black leather gloves and a black cycle cap. Henry, who had sharp features, had pulled the material on the cap forward and had sewn it to the bill, which kept it from blousing up in the wind (but it did not keep it from flying off at speed). I loved the Langlitz jacket but was not fond of the Harley jacket, which had a large collar that continued down the front. I sold the Harley jacket to John Farlow for $10.00, so the whole outfit—Langlitz jacket, wedge-bottom boots, cap and gloves—cost me only $10.00!

Roy Burke on his BSA on the sand. Note engineer boots with steel toe, leather pants, cap and goggles (no crash helmet).

The Morning Speed Run

       Tickle it twice
       a little throttle
       down hard on compression stroke

       and if it don't kick back break your leg
       it'll start:

       the sharp bark/ open exhaust
       snuffy off
       TT carb won't idle but it'll crank man

       like this Beezer
       has a switch:
       OFF and ON

June/ early morning/ a cool mist hangs in sunlight
on a day like this the exhaust cracks sharp and fine
it's tuned/ the light smell of oil boiling off cooling fins
gas sloshing in the tank/ the glare of chrome fire

english jacket zipped to the neck/ no collar/levis
around the grips gloves fit fingers like a film of grease wedge boots/ skid
plate/ hotshoe bike-jockey leadfoot
tip the sharp-billed cap which flies off at sixty

       clutch in
       toe tips the gear lever
       up

       throttle back
       ease the clutch out

       and the knobby grabs
       spins gravel
       down the driveway
       into the road

       motion/ moving/ getting away

Riding Bike in the Fifties

      grab a handful and hang on
      wind it out
      clutch in/ toe down/ hang second
      the front wheel lifting

      gone

balance/ the chrome tank held by knees/ leaning
the flat bars an extension of arms/ leaning/ guiding forks
lay it over/ seat of the pants sensing motion/ movement
wind it out/ tight/ rpm's sweeping toward the redline
exhaust ringing the high notes of anarchy/ gone

      back off/ clutch
      toe down to third

      wind ripping
      against the forehead
      a gale size of a fifty cent piece

      toe down to fourth
      the road slides past
      a blur/ the flash of traffic

      aimed over flat bars
      toward that hard uncertain horizon

flat out/ exhaust a note of anarchy through the high-pipe
echoing/ breaking/ shattering against the peaceful landscape
cows moving away from fences/ farmers shaking fists

moving/ going/ gone   freeeeeee

Bikes on display at Speed-O-Rama, Portland's second hot rod show, March, 1952 at the Portland Auditorium.

Bonneville Salt Flats, 1955.

Paul Watts

Murdersickling in the Fifties; it was a new, exciting world for us hayseed kids out at Corbett. Leroy Brenneke was the first to get one—an AJS 30.50 single around 1953-54. Oh, it was a wicked machine: black tank, side covers, fenders, with gold leaf striping, and it was the fastest vehicle any of us farm kids had ever seen. Leroy dressed the part too, 'black leather jacket with an eagle on the back'—yeah, just like the song; Langlitz leathers made him the envy of the rest of us punks in high school. Next was Jerry Gravett with an old K-model Harley, and Tony Angelo one-upped them all with a new Gold Star. None of us had even seen a new motorcycle before.

I bought a 1947 Indian vertical single. Thought I was hot stuff until I blew it up at 40 mph. Oil and shards of metal lay all over Hurlburt Road when a drunken Italian came along in a gorgeous 1941 Ford four door, stopped, and hollered out, "Whasamatta? Sickle gone gunnysack?" We stuffed the broken Injun into the back seat of that Ford, took it up to the farm, and he hooked the rear door on a tree in my driveway, which folded the back door into the body. It didn't bother the old drunk though: "Sumbitch ain't hurt a bit." That nice '41 Ford was irreparably injured, but no one seemed to care.

One night the four of us punks were cruising Sandy Boulevard in Tony Angelo's father's '51 Chevrolet Powerglide, and we started smarting off to some guy in a '50 Merc. He was quite mannerly about the unpleasant encounter, but suggested we follow him to his house so he could get his other car. He led us to an old house near Franklin High, where we saw the "other car", a 1939 Ford, primered and lowered—a typical hot rod under construction, which we knew we could beat with Leroy's screaming AJS. Well, he followed us out to Leroy's house on Bell Grade near Springdale, and we went to Corbett to run 'er off from the grade school past the high school. We had ridiculed the guy so much and acted like such fools, and we were set to enjoy victory. It didn't happen; the AJS did a beautiful wheelie coming off the line, but that flathead Ford waxed us like a speeding bullet; it was brutal. Were we ashamed? Rightly so, especially after he told us what he had in it: every piece of speed equipment a flathead could hold, which we should have known when we heard the starter just barely turn it over—harrumph, harrumph, harrumph—so extreme was the compression. He told us how badly he could trounce Jags and everything else brave enough to take him on, and we had a very un-merry serving of humble pie as we apologized.

Motorcycling was such fun back then: no helmet laws, no lights-on, no special driver's license, no insurance, and we seldom even licensed the bikes themselves. There were practically no cops out there in those days, so we really had no effective check on our *laissez faire* recklessness out in the country.

I should mention the short-lived Corbett Ridge Runners and the sporadic hill climbs at Hubbard's Hill. Bert Hubbard, his wife, and a passel of kids lived in a shack at the top of a really steep hill just east of Corbett; around the place were some old cars, including a 1937 Packard, in which some of the kids slept, and a menagerie of decrepit old Harleys shared space with goats and chickens in the broken-down shanty that passed for a barn.

Once in a while riders would gather at the bottom of the hill in the pasture to attack the hill on their AJs, or Triumphs, BSAs, or whatever they could scrounge up that would run; this was in the late 1950s, well before the current rash of specialized hill-climbers bikes that have made such sport easy for weekend professionals. Nay, back then everybody had to "run what they brung", and what they brung were just street bikes, and no one really knew anything about the since-refined techniques of booming up a hill and over the top–especially there, for a bunch of old shacks and cars were just beyond the crest of the hill, so anyone who successfully made it up that vertical incline had to beware the obstacles that awaited.

Hubbard's Hill was totally unstructured: no price of admission, no rules, no insurance prohibitions, no mandatory helmets, no prizes, no cops or security guards, just absolute freedom to do as you wished. Early on, there were just us local ne'er-do-wells who were friends of old Bert, but later on people started riding out from faraway places like Gresham, and the Ridge Runners somehow came into being as a totally unregulated, loosely connected group; I doubt that it lasted much beyond the mid 1960s. Bert eventually died, the kids grew up and moved out of the cars, and the property changed hands. My last visit was in 1967, when I rode out on my new BSA Lightning on my first date with the girl who later became my wife (and still is).

There was always lots of beer around in those carefree days at the climb; there was nothing unusual about a rider barreling up the hill and crashing from pulling a DUII between pasture and crest. I don't think anyone ever got hurt, though; they just rolled off and sobered up enough to try 'er again. Liability lawyers? What's that?

On that climb in '67, Bert got his old 80-inch flathead running somehow, downed his day's quota of beer, and came roaring up the hill pedal-to-the-metal, bounced over the crest and crashed headlong into the goat shed. Suddenly the air was full of broken lumber, the cacophony of squawking chickens and angry goats as Bert drunkenly untangled himself from animals, motorcycle, and shed, and staggered out, full enjoying the show as much as we who were watching.

O, the times we had.

Incident

Perhaps that's the wrong title, since an incident is a small event, even trivial. Perhaps this piece should have been called, "The Day I Could Have Died." That's how I view it today, although when it happened it was an incident, just one of the crazy things that happened every day when I was growing up. And not just to me—stuff happened to most of my car buddies, whether it was a busted transmission or a speeding ticket or a pregnant girlfriend or worse. We were all crazy.

There is a place in Portland, Oregon where three major streets intersect—Sandy Boulevard, Burnside and 12th Avenue—in a confusion of traffic lights. The city has declared it the worst intersection, and it was not much better fifty years ago, when traffic was reasonable. Recently I was standing in a parking lot, once the site of the Tik Tok, a notable drive-in restaurant, looking at that intersection and I had a revelation about something that had happened there, something that seems important but that I had totally forgot.

From 1953 to 1955 I worked in a garage located about half a mile from where I was standing. I remembered that one day, shortly before closing, I had to make a parts run to pick up something small, such as set of points or a carburetor repair kit. I figured, why take the truck, I'll just run down on my cycle. I had a gorgeous 1951 BSA Gold Star, and I was always looking for a reason to ride it.

Next to the garage was a service station where I sometimes worked, and the kid who was working there that day had recently come up from California on a Triumph Thunderbird. I can't remember the details, but for some reason I rode his bike to the store. Did he urge me? Did I ask? That's odd, since I had grown wary of jumping on strange bikes, every one was different. I learned that lesson when I tried out a Matchless twin that a neighborhood kid was trying to sell. It was an original cycle with all road equipment and appeared to be in nice shape. I cruised on the side streets until I came to a T intersection, and I found that the bike had no brakes! Nothing! There wasn't time to kick it down a couple gears! In those days in my neighborhood there were no curbs or sidewalks, which was a good thing because I shot right over where they would have been, through a yard, across a driveway, through another yard and back out on the street! I slowly rode it out to the owner's house and parked it.

Maybe I had not learned a lesson, because I got on that Thunderbird and everything was different. The handlebars were a foot wider than I was used to, and that 40-inch twin had a different kind of power than my 30.50 single. The biggest difference was the foot shift; my BSA was up for low, then down three times, and the Triumph was the exact opposite. I moved into traffic which, since it was nearly five o'clock, was beginning to pick up, got through that bad intersection and got to the Stevens Company where I picked up the part and headed back.

I went a short block to Burnside and, still in low, turned right, staying in the outside lane. That Thunderbird had lots of torque and long gears, and I

Incident

shifted up, into second, and moved up the hill. I wanted to turn left on Sandy, which meant I had to get in a left turn lane pronto. I decided I could rip ahead of traffic and make a fairly illegal left turn, so I cranked on the throttle and that big Triumph responded.

Everything might've been okay, but in the heat of the moment I did a dumb thing. I was moving quickly, and from habit I shifted downward, which put that Triumph back in first gear! Of course at that same moment I grabbed a handful of throttle. That bike leaped forward, engine screaming, the front wheel lifted a considerable distance and I thought I was going over backwards. I felt a sense of stupidity and helplessness, which I've experienced in various situations, but in this one I could have been killed. I figured the bike would go over backwards or the engine would blow or I'd run into that turkey ahead of me. I think I was airborne clear through the intersection and I had plenty of time—probably two seconds—to consider how hard that pavement was. Perhaps I visualized a bloody spot on the asphalt. In those days no one wore a crash helmet.

I came down, turned left, rode carefully back to the station and returned the bike. Neither it nor I got hurt, which is why this was an incident rather than a tragedy. It's a story with a happy ending. But, looking back, I realize how young, how invincible, invulnerable, how daring we were, and how little good sense we had. Okay, I'll just speak for myself: when I consider things I did as a teenager I question my judgment and lack of maturity. I think that until I was 21 I should not have had a sharp knife, a firearm, any amount of money over $20 or a girlfriend. Especially, I should not have had a motorcycle. But I'm glad I did.

I took this photo of unidentified Triumph motorcycle at Madras, Oregon ¾ mile timed runs in 1952.

Riding Bike in the Fifties

Riding Bike in the Fifties

Bonneville 1955: I had a BSA Gold Star, and was nuts about cycles. A bunch of them were running, and again I saw names I knew from magazines: Bud Hare, Joe Simpson, Bus Schaller, Marty Dickerson on the first Vincent I'd ever seen, and the Brute, built by Chet Herbert. The Texas Cigar was running with its streamlined body and, I think, two Triumph motors. Pat Conolly, the noted cam grinder from Portland, was running a Triumph. A guy from the Midwest (Robert Bud Schmitt, above) was running a lengthened chassis with two Harley Davidson motors; it was aptly called The Monster.

What We Rode

    Beezers/ Gold Stars
    Velocettes/ Ariels
    AJS/ Matchless
    Royal-Enfields
    Triumphs:
    Cub
    Tiger
    Trophy
    T-Bird
    a few Nortons
    Vincent Black Shadows
    Moto-Guzzi/ NSU

    no jap bikes at all except the British JAP
    Harleys/ Indians
    but they were a different
    breed/ hogs/ pavement cowboys
    drive-in racers
    hundreds of lights/ radio
    turn signals/ fox tails
    mudflaps/ cigaret lighters
    these guys wore Harley caps
    sported mustaches
    claimed they were
    cleaning up the sport

there weren't so many bikes really/ only seemed like more
you could ride a whole day and not see another motor
unless you knew where to look/ so few bikes when we met
we waved/ and it meant something/ brothers/ comrades
the fraternity of fools/ we knew we were special
allied/ set apart from those with four wheels
or no wheels at all

    poppers/ one lungers
    twins/ square fours
    thirty-fifties/ 500cc's
    forty cubes/ 650cc's
    forty cubes/ 650cc's
    big fours/ 1000cc's

Riding Bike in the Fifties

plungers/ rigid frames
swinging arms/ flat bars
A bars/ J bars
knobbies/ grasshoppers
trials universal
baldies/ suicide rubber

buy a new bike in the spring/ low down payment
a little a month/ new paint/ gears/ chrome/ buddy seat
sleek tank/ chain links fit teeth like a glove
you never figured to own it/ nor it own you
run it hard all summer/ balls out/ cross-country/ climbs
and turn it back in the fall/ the hell with the equity

Alan Tessman raced his Triumph at drag strip ad Bonneville salt flats. Note spring hub.

Race Ace

GARY DAVIS

Gary Davis

I used to go trailing on my friend's motorcycle at Oregon Shipyard, and one of the guys there was Glenn Wright. I could beat him hands down, and he said why don't you come out to our local track, the Sidewinders. Well, I did, and that did it; that hooked me. At that time we were racing little Triumph Cubs, and the big boy was Bill Donaca. He was the one to beat. After I got to beating him and got to be number one in that class the Sandy Bandit (Cliff Majhor) said, I just took this bike away from Sonny Burres, would you race it for me? A 500cc Triumph. I went out there and started winning with that and I kept on with it. Then Triumph started helping me.

I won because I was real good at getting off the line. Getting up front right away, and holding it. Real good at that. The only guy who was even close to me was Eddie Mulder, down in the L.A. area. He was a good starter too, but I was just a little quicker. That was my bag. I think at that little track at Sidewinders I always remember that was my big secret.

That was a fun time. All of your old friends would sit down there at the bottom of the track drinking all that beer. Remember all that beer those people would drink? Unreal! Come back with big flats of beer, from the beer stand. I think they must have had two or three beer stands at Sidewinders. In fact my cousin was one of the Sidewinders, also a longshoreman, he said, hell, that's how we paid for everything, with the beer sales. Those were the days. All gone.

I broke my ankle badly up in Washington, on a half mile. That and a collar bone and jeez I was a mess. I just said that's enough. They started talking about amputating the foot and I thought oh no. At the time all I had was a bathtub, I didn't have a shower, and I thought god that'd be terrible laying in that bathtub scrubbing that stump. That did it. I quit smoking cigarettes that day and I quit motorcycle racing. Of course, I stayed heavily involved by sponsoring guys. I had been fortunate enough to have several of the best of the best that were riding my bikes. Out of California I had Ricky Graham, up here I had Chuck Joyner, he raced for me right to the end, and Randy Scott, and Hank Scott, who was Gary Scott's brother out of California, he got national number 14—that was the national number I got—and then I sponsored him. Those guys were all faster than me. It was fun. Still is.

I never rode on the street. Never did, other than a few times on these cruises to the motorcycle shops, or that the clubs would have. I raced for Harley-Davidson for a while, the East Side Motorcycle shop, and they would have these things. I did that a few times, but other than that I never rode on the street. Too many friends were getting hurt and killed. Of course, I always had a car, usually a nice car. To get to a place to ride I'd throw the bike in the trunk of a car. Eventually we all had El Caminos to carry cycles, and we all went to vans. We had the vans for a long, long time.

I don't remember Indian Rock, but I rode Mt. Scott. Get there and meet friends, they'd invite you and and you'd go riding. The Tillamook Burn down

Gary Davis

here, where I eventually moved to, that was the place. That was it, boy. We had our group, a whole bunch. We kept a cabin out at Lee's Camp out here and I was riding here every chance I got. Of course, I was racing in those days and riding in the Burn was a damn good practice. Kept you on your toes.

I belonged to a club, it used to meet at my house. I never joined the Sidewinder club, even though a lot of the members were longshoremen and friends of mine. I was always building, I loved to build engines, and I was building my own bikes, and those of friends, and everybody in the country. In those days I was divorced, and had a home with a swimming pool, and that was crazy. That was the hangout. I'd be out there working on those bikes, and go to work on the waterfront. At home there were a lot of people hanging around. It got crazy! There were a lot of women too, especially because of the swimming pool. That was the deal. Gale Britton was one of my roommates. They were good times.

I raced flat tracks, that was my main thing. I got a national number, number 14. When I started out we ran without brakes, but then they implemented a rear brake and they still do. We ran 500cc Triumphs and 500cc BSAs and so forth in the Novice class. Then you jumped into the 750cc deal, which they still do. Gene Thiessen usually raced a 500cc Gold Star, and he was absolutely great. There were a lot of them from here, Red Rice, Elden Wright was damn good, a whole bunch. Then it went through a period of also rans, and then now, the fast racers are back again. I've already bought tickets for the Grand National Mile at Sacramento this year, and for Santa Rosa. I'm sponsoring a couple guys. I'm heavily involved.

Gary Davis at the track.

Billy Zerbach's 1950 Triumph 500cc. twin. New owner removed the megaphones, put on "pencil tip" exhaust pipes. (1956)

Bill Zerbach

I bought my motorcycle from a guy named Gordon Crook. His folks had a florist business here in Roseburg, and when he got married his wife said he had to sell it. He wrecked it going over to the coast and he had it repaired, all fixed up. It came out of a dealership in Eugene. The guy put these riser pipes, that come up and go under your legs, it had big megaphones, and riser bars. On the Triumph it had that little thing on the top of the gas tank, had little chrome bars in it. I don't know what it was for, they leaded that off and painted the bike, recovered the seats in white Naugahyde, it was just fixed up really neat. It was a 1950, with the spring hub in the rear. I got it in 1955 for $500 and sold it in 1956. A friend of mine, Gary Burkhardt, had a 500cc Triumph, and he said he knew where there was a cycle for sale and he took me down there. I told the owner I'd buy it but I'd have to make payments, and he said that's okay, so I just took money to him whenever I got paid.

We never liked to ride with the Harley riders and they wanted us to ride with them; we'd take off and go around three corners and lose them. We could lay those things over. They had a real narrow tire in front, about an inch wide and then they tapered on each side, you could really lay those things into the corners. We'd ride off and lose those Harley guys! We called them hogs. How fast that hog go? What'd you feed those hogs? we'd say. What are those saddle bags for, you got acorns for your hogs?

I did some dumb things on it. I was out of high school, I was 18, but I ate lunch there. I was in the parking lot and this kid just had to have a ride on my cycle. We went out on the North Umpqua, a two lane road, it was paved all the way to Glide, and we were going about 80 mph, there was a log truck ahead of me and another coming from the other direction and I went right between the two of them, when they were side by side, going in opposite directions. I had been going 70 and I cranked it wide open and passed. I gave that kid a ride! Then I rode ahead and kind of hid until those trucks were gone. Those drivers were mad!

It made a lot of noise. I had straight pipes on it with those big megaphones. I took all the guts out. In the photo, the guy I sold it to put on pencil tips, because I kind of curled up the megaphones. I was doing a wheelie and it got away from me, curled up the rear fender and the megaphones.

Another day, I had to show up at the driver's license bureau, and they told me that if I get one more ticket they were going to take my license. On the way home, I had an old '40 Ford I'd bought and I put the transmission in my '40 coupe, because the transmission was bad. I had it in the '40 and I blew the case and everything up, blew it up, it broke the case into pieces. So I went home and got on my motorcycle and came back to town. I was working at the mill, I had to go to work at 4:30, 5:00 o'clock, and I was on my way home, on Harvard, and I was rattling the windows downtown. I never saw this cop. There was a school bus that was stopped, right by the fire station, on the hill. I had to stop for it, there were three or four cars ahead of me. I looked back; the cop didn't have his lights on. I just rolled around past these cars. I followed behind the school bus, it went to another stop, then turned up Looking Glass Hill. I just cut it loose when it turned and we lived about a mile up that road. I got about half a mile and a spark plug wire came off and I ran out of gas. I coasted up the hill, and I was going so fast I almost missed the driveway and lost the bike. I rode into the yard, parked the bike behind my dad's truck, jumped the fence and laid down in the tall grass. They'd seen me turn off, so they pulled in and mom was just coming out of the house. They said, did you see a motorcycle, did it turn in here? And she said, Well, it must've, it's right over there! I'm laying out there in the bushes listening to this, but I had to get to work. And dad had to take me, because the cycle didn't have a headlight. And it didn't have a front fender.

Anyway I was laying down there a long time, and the cop just stayed there. I heard him call for a search warrant, he thought I was in the house. I decided I couldn't wait longer, I'd just walk up there and see what happens. Well, they took me to jail. The cop said I've gotta take you in. For what? I asked. Reckless driving, he said. He said he'd clocked me between these two streets. You did not, I said. One street was where I'd stopped for the school bus. He said he'd clocked me at 70 mph. They got me for reckless driving. They didn't charge me with eluding an officer, I don't know why. I got an attorney and they agreed to give me a license so I could go back and forth to work and to drop my $75.00 fine down to $50.00.

There were a fair number of motorcycles in Roseburg then. Bev (his wife) had two cousins who rode 500cc BSA twins, and there was another kid, Tom Dentley, he had a cycle, and Gary Burkhardt had one. And a guy came from Hawaii and he had a 650cc Triumph, it was souped up more than mine. He and I and Gary rode together a lot. We just rode on the street. We rarely went trail riding, it wasn't very good for that, a BSA single was better. The Triumphs had more power, but not much traction and they'd just spin out.

There was a cycle club in town, the Roseburg Rumble Bees. They were trying to get me to join, but that article came out in the paper, about my reckless driving ticket. Tom Dentley, he was working for the *News Review*, putting the paper together, and he went in and talked them into toning it down a little bit. He was afraid they wouldn't let me in the Rumble Bees. Well, I didn't want to join anyway—they were hog riders.

There were quite a few Harleys in town. Once I was coming across the Umpqua River, it was a steel bridge, with that grid pattern, and oh man that thing would really echo off the bridge. I went around a couple corners and there was a city cop—they did have a couple cycle cops—and he pulled me over. He used to do a lot of parades. He said, look, I know this thing is illegal, I'm not going to write you a ticket. Any of the other cops would have written me a ticket, but he was a motorcyclist, he had his own motorcycle as well as the one he rode for the city.

There was no motorcycle shop in Roseburg then, but Tom Dentley did repairs in his garage. Later, he was too smart to take on the Honda, he took on the Suzuki! Bev's cousin had a Harley, and his best friend had a Harley, a '37, I think, and his dad had a machine shop. I used to ride with them quite a bit. Two brothers had Harleys, then they bought BSA twins. We were going up to Looking Glass Road, the one guy was telling everybody that he passed me, trying to make me mad, and I got right behind him on the corners, and the kickstand on that BSA was underneath the frame, and he caught it on a corner and I was about three inches from him and I went around him. It pushed him sideways. I don't know how I kept from hitting him but I cranked it on and passed him in third gear, then I kicked it into fourth gear and went off and left him there.

It rained so much then, the weather was really crappy. It's changed now. When you went over the O Street bridge, I went over it once on a cycle and slid clear across, it scared the crap out of me, I never went across it again in the rain. Another kid had a '56 Triumph and he wrecked it on that bridge. That was before I was riding. There were quite a few cycles around when I think about it.

I was kind of a terror. I wore Levis, black T-shirt, and white buck shoes that I dyed black. I did that because I had a little oil leak back where my gear shift was and that made a grease spot and I couldn't get it off my shoe so I dyed them black! Remember that song that came out about then, "Terror of Highway 101"? Well, this girl I was going out with then, her mother said, every time I hear that song I think of you. I wore a leather jacket in the winter, a brown leather jacket, the kind that was popular when we were in high school.

I went up to Portland and was going to buy a new Harley Scrambler. It was at a Triumph shop on Union or off Union, and I got on this bike and I was just cracking the throttle wide open, I was trying the bike out, it was a brand new bike, and I pulled out of the lot onto a four lane road, and when I hit the center, there was gravel in it, and I come so close to losing that bike it scared the crap out of me! But I never let off and it pulled me through it. Dick Emra and his brother were with me. You don't need a motorcycle, they said, you're going to kill yourself.

My Triumph had a real narrow front tire, and the front fender had been removed, and the front tire made it look like a Whizzer. One time I came around this corner in Roseburg where you're going west, then you head north for one block, then you head right back west again and then you went into a tunnel under the freeway. This guy had about a '52 or '53 Chevrolet, and I was being a smart ass. We were stopped at the light and I looked at him two or three times, and I had it at an idle, I'm just barely tickling the throttle, and I was down like I was pushing it along, like it was a Whizzer. I could see him grab his steering wheel and push that gas pedal as far down as it would go on that Chevrolet. About that time I lit it up, and I went through that tunnel, and it just roared. That guy tried to kill me! He was trying to run over me!

Another time, I was coming home in my '40 Ford, and Bev's cousin was behind me on my motorcycle, and went under that same bridge and when we went into that same corner he just cranked it on and passed and he was gone, he was way ahead of me. When I went through that tunnel that noise was still rapping in there, and it scared the shit out of me! It was so loud! No wonder that guy was trying to kill me! You couldn't believe the noise that cycle made. I used to go with a girl in high school and I'd park there, I was out of school then, and this one teacher, his room was near the road. When the bell rang and everybody went into the classrooms, this one English teacher would say, well, as soon as Mr. Zerbach starts his bike up and does his thing we'll get class started. The kids said it just rattled the windows in the room!

Bev was in the drum corps—this was before I knew her—and they used to march in Portland all the time. All girls. One time they were marching in Roseburg, and I had this kid on the cycle behind me, and they were marching down the main street, they took up the whole street. This kid on the back was jumping up and down on the pegs, yelling, go, go, go. I'd of never done it, but he coaxed me into it, and I cranked it on and roared between the two lines of girls. The drum major was a guy, kind of a midget guy, he was an old guy and I think he was a midget. He looked after his girls and he didn't put up with any nonsense, he got mad at guys all the time. It's a wonder that he didn't ask the girls who was on that cycle, because they knew. This guy that was on behind me, just as we got past the girls, he kind of turned around and kicked one foot up in the air and yells, Heeeeee-haaaw, and I damn near dumped him. It was funny.

Sidewinders of Oregon

If there is one group of the racing fraternity that can put on a show it's the bikes. Here are some of the Sidewinders going full tilt into a turn.

61 Ray Carroll, 69 Roger Betnar, 62 Ross Aylett, 13 Dave Bacus, 48Q Bill Burke, 63, Cecil Johnson (Photograph by Frank Clay)

Sidewinders

In 1954 I had a 1947 BSA twin and my friend Bob Kaseweter had a 1951 BSA 30.50 single. On Saturdays I had to work half a day in the garage and after lunch I'd ride out Powell to Southeast 136th, which was where Bob lived. His neighbors to the north were two longshoremen who lived in adjoining houses; one guy, I think, was named Jimmy Hubbard. This was a rough and tumble neighborhood, and it did not seem odd that these guys had turned their back yards into a small race track simply by riding their motorcycles around and around in an oval until there was no grass, only mud.

> **Cyclers to Race On Muddy Oval**
>
> The Oregon Sidewinders' motorcycle club, a group which favors racing in the slipperiest mud possible, will hold a regular race program Sunday on the club track, at S. E. 82d and Lawnfield road.
>
> Approximately 40 entrants are expected for the event, which begins with time trials at 11:30 a. m. The track is located six miles south of S. E. Foster.

I cranked it on around the track but my twin was so unresponsive it was no race. Another guy cut around me on the outside, stayed on the throttle into the end curve and went off the track, drove a couple feet up a board fence and came back down to the track; the evidence was the muddy tire track that went up, then down, the fence boards. If that was a race, I lost. Bob remembers that he was cranking it on when one guy began to pass on the outside. Then Archie Stanley decided to go between the two cycles! They were handlebar to handlebar, and that's when Bob decided to back off.

Jimmy Hubbard, Archie Stanley and a few other guys pooled their money and bought a large chunk of land south of Sunnyside Road; that was out in the country in 1955. They built a race course, more Hound and Hare than a flat track, and since their club was called the Sidewinders it was called the Sidewinders track. To get there you drove east on Sunnyside Road, which in those days was a two lane road, then turned right on Lawnfield Road, which was a muddy, bumpy, narrow road. It led to a large field, often covered with knee-high grass. Then there were some homemade grandstands, a concession stand and toilets. The track, as I recall, was laid out on the side of a hill, with the start/finish line at the bottom. The track went uphill, then turned left and went uphill more until it reached its zenith, then repeated itself on the way down. The final descent was steep, and it made for a thrill-packed race.

One of the guys who raced at the Sidewinders track when it opened in 1956 was Keith Preskey. He began knowing nothing about cycle racing and became a successful racer. "I got started when I bought this bike from a guy, a 30.50 BSA. I was riding down 82nd to Roy's Tavern and I ran into some motorcyclists. They said, Okay, we're going over to Eastside Motorcycle shop and they'll have a big parade out to Sidewinders. I rode to Eastside and there were 200 or 300 bikes there. That was the Harley dealer. They planned a big opening day race, on a Saturday, and they'd have this big parade out to the track.

Sidewinders

So I rode out to Sidewinders and somebody said why don't you race that BSA? I said I've just started riding, I've never raced. But I entered that day and I got hooked. On that cycle I didn't do too bad, and then I got another one. There was a Darrel Coates I worked with at Hudson House and he used to mix fuel for the guys out at Portland Speedway and Jantzen Beach for their race cars. So he mixed me up some fuel for my 30.50 BSA and I was beating 40 inchers. They'd tear me down and couldn't find anything illegal. Maybe they didn't know how to check fuels then.

"Then I went to a 40 inch BSA twin and I didn't like that. So I went to the Harley shop and they talked me into racing for them. I bought a 45 inch Harley and I raced that. I did good with the Harley, won a lot. Then I went to

Triumph, a TT special. I was never scared at Sidewinders. I'd come down that last hill and I was one of those guys who'd kick the wheels out from other riders. I was kind of crazy. I'd knock them over. They knew if they were on the inside of me on that first turn they'd better back off on the throttle or they'd go down in the pits. I'd just pull over and hit their front wheel and knock 'em off. But it was fun and I met a lot of nice people. John Farlow, Gene Curry. Actually I'd known those guys at Franklin High. I knew Gene when he used to ride a Whizzer in front of my house and my dog would chase him, bite his heels, and he'd kick at him. I told him one time, you kick my dog and I'm going to kick your ass! One day he came by and kicked my dog and I ran out there and grabbed him, knocked him off his bike and I almost poked him in the nose! He became a top cycle mechanic and tuner, and one of the best racers. He worked for Jackie Leigh out on 82nd —him and Farlow both, they ran that shop. That's who I bought my Triumph TT special from.

"It was fun. You raced at the Sidewinders on Friday night and go to Spot 79. Take the wife, go with a bunch of people. I'd make enough money racing to buy a T-bone, a baked potato and have a few drinks.

"Roy Burke came out but he didn't race—he'd quit racing by then. He and Hubert Simon had Allied Cycle at 37th and Powell. Cliff Majhor, the Sandy Bandit, he had the Triumph shop on Sandy Boulevard. He was racing when I first started – he used to race at Hare and Hounds. Burke and Simon too. That'd be around 1954, '55.

"Every Saturday we'd meet at Roy's Tavern on 82nd about a block and a half south of the Checkered Flag Tavern (at Flavel). We'd drink beer and go riding at Indian Rock, then on up Mt. Scott. We'd take a couple cases of beer and go up there to Deardorf Road and Top 'O Scott and ride for about five hours and never hit the same trail.

"Sometimes we'd hang out at Merhar's—that was my favorite hamburger place. Hamburgers and milkshakes, they had the best milkshakes in town. We'd go to The Speck for French fries but if we wanted a hamburger we'd go to Merhar's.

"We also used to ride at Swan Island, out there by Kelly Point, in St. Johns. That was a good place, it was all sand dunes. No roads. We'd have these little Enduro type races; you'd race around and around the course.

"I raced on a few flat racks. We went down to Sacramento. A miler. We used to load our bikes up and take off, go down to California. They'd come up here and they'd do halfway decent, but we beat a lot of the California guys. We'd go down there and we'd beat some of them, but the real hotshots knew their tracks.

"I raced against Gary Davis, he was a buddy of mine, we were both longshoremen. John Farlow was one of the best. They called him 'Sliding John'. I knew Mort Becker, he was a good friend of mine. He was a starter at Sidewinders. So was old man Donaca. I had them down pat. I knew when they'd drop the flag. They had a little twitch, kind of twist a little muscle in their neck. I'd go watch the starter before every race and they'd all have a little quirk. Some

Sidewinders

of them would drop their shoulder, just a little, the arm that held the flag, just before they dropped the flag. Well, when they dropped their shoulder I'd drop my clutch, and when they dropped the flag I was on my way! I did that with Donaca too. He had a little twitch, and he'd kinda tighten his lip up, and the muscle under his neck would tighten up, and when he dropped the flag I was already on my way!

26 Ron Klemp, 98 Bob Christner, 30, Keith Presky, 3 Jack Stafford
(Photograph by Frank Clay)

"At Sidewinders they had had bales to sit on at first, and then they built bleachers. The wives would sit together and they'd drink bottles of Thunderbird wine. Then the Sidewinders began selling beer, and they sold more kegs of beer on a Friday night than most taverns did in a month.

"They hired off duty Clackamas County Sheriffs for security, and the cops got drunk out there too. One cop got a guy's wife pregnant. The guy was a longshoreman, and he was one of the guys who got Sidewinders track started. A Clackamas County Sheriff knocked his wife up! He was hired by Sidewinders to keep order, and while the husband was working on the track the cop took the wife out in the parking lot and had sex with her. Got her pregnant!

"Sidewinders was a club as well as a race track. We met at that old rock house next to the track. We had a caretaker there. He made wine and he liked me so he'd take me out in the kitchen during meetings and give me some of his home made wine. He made dandelion wine, rhubarb wine, blackberry wine. They let him live there. He gave me some old wooden wine kegs and taught me how to make blackberry wine.

"I was in Sidewinders with Ray Celorie. I went to high school with Ray—Franklin. He had a bike but he never raced. Ray always acted like a tough guy but I never did see him fight anybody. Everybody was scared of him because he had such a mouth on him. He never was intimidating to me but some people were scared to death of him. He divorced his wife to marry this other lady and when that lady was going to divorce him he went and shot himself.

"Those Hare and Hounds were fun. The Tindall brothers, Don and Ron, they'd quit racing just before I got started, but they sponsored guys at Sidewinders. Guys like Sonny Burres. When I first started there was Crazy Leo, and Archie Stanley, the Gypsy, who had the Norton shop on 82nd. Crazy Leo rode for Archie. In those days every shop sponsored somebody. Then I won number one in the northwest and number four in the nation that year, which was 1965. That was my last year of racing. They put me and Vern Lundquist, a friend of mine, on the front page of the program. Me and John Holman, we were fighting neck and neck. He ran around with that guy who broke his back out there (at Sidewinders). He worked for John. John had a Triumph that year (in 1965) and we were fighting it out for the championship. I beat him out. In fact, I didn't even have to ride the last race and I won it. It was fun, but then guys broke their backs, and a guy name Dick Jagow got killed at a run over in Bend, and there were other things I wanted to do so I decided to quit. I raced for 10 years. After I had my good year, number one in the northwest, number four in the nation, amateur, I decided well I couldn't go much higher, so I quit."

23 Bruce Stoner, Number 1 rider for 1962 (Photograph by Frank Clay)

OREGON SIDEWINDERS MOTORCYCLE CLUB, INC.

Name and Number of Riders for 1963

Top Riders of the Year

15 Inch — Fred Roentz   30-50 Inch Dave Bacus   40 Inch Bruce Stoner

No.	Name	No.	Name	No.	Name
1	BRUCE STONER	54	CLIFF ANDERSON	107	JIM GOOCH
2	FRED ROENTZ	55	JERRY CHAPMAN	108	
3	JACK STAFFORD	56	BOB TUCKER	109	
	DAVE BACUS	57	EARL DAILEY	110	LLOYD ZIMMERMAN
5	JIM MOORE	58	ART BAKER	111	
6	BILL DONACA	59	STEVE GIMARELLI	112	
7	BILL OLIVER	60	DENNIS SEIFERT	113	
8	BOB WATSON	61	RUSSELL COMSTOCK	114	
9	KEN NEWMAN	62	BILL TOMAN	115	
10	GARY GARDNER	63	C. J. JOHNSON	116	
11	DAN DONACA	64	DICK GREENSLITT	117	DELBERT R WITT
12	STAN JOHNSON	65	VIC STANKEWITSCH	118	
13	LOU BURTIS	66	BOB JENSEN	119	
14	JAY GORDON, JR	67	JOHN WILLIAMS	120	
15	DOC SCOFIELD	68	LEO PLUMBLEY	121	
16	DENNIS ASH Y	69	GARRY FERGUSON	122	
17	JIM DAVIS	70	VERN LUNDQUIST	123	
18	BOB MERDITH	71	BOB JOYNER	124	
19	ROSS AYLETT	72	BOB PARTLOW	125	
20	RAY GUSTAVICH	73	JACK JOYNER	126	VIRGIL WILSON
21	DICK JAGOW	74	LARRY JOHNSON	127	
22	T L HOGLAN	75	JACK HUGHES	128	
23	MELVIN SMITH	76	CLAUDE MOSER	129	
24	TOM PAPST	77	WALLY GRIFFIN	130	
25	JOHN TAYLOR	78	FLOYD JOHNSON	131	
26	RON KLEMP	79		132	
27	ARILE ENGLER	80		133	
28	JIM BROWNLEE	81		134	
29	BOB ROLLER	82		135	
30	KEITH PRESKY	83		136	
31	ED RICHARDSON	84		137	
32	TED CHRISTENSEN	85	MATHEW McKEE	138	
33	GARY JEAN	86		139	
34	CLAUD WEAVER	87		140	
35	DICK LALICKER	88		141	
36	ROBIN HARRISON	89		142	
37	LEE LEWIS	90	HAROLD MEREDITH	143	
38	DON MOE	91	RON QUICK	144	
39	JIM LANCASTER	92		145	
40	NORMAN DODGE	93		146	
41	DEL BURGESS	94	JIM SMITH	147	
42	BILL PARTLOW	95		148	
43	JIM D. TALLMAN	96		151	JIM WHITE
44	BILL SCOTT	97		226	JOE MARIES
45	JOHN HIGGINS	98	BOB CHRISTNER	227	JACK COTTERMAN
46	PAUL PITTELKO	99		228	GENE DIMICK
47	WALLACE MAY	100	JIM SHEPPARD	229	WAYNE VAUGHN
48	JIM BARTKOWSKI	101	JIM WILLOCK	230	JIM MORGANSON
49	VIC SMITH	102		231	WALT MADSEN
50	RODGER BETNAR	103		350	BOB GOURLEY
51	RAY CARROL	104		351	MORRIS PORTIN
52	ERNIE WAGAMAN	105	MERLE LARSON	352	JACK DINGES
53	BOB WRIGHT	106		711	R K LAMARCHE

Name and Number of Riders of 50CC Motors

No.	Name	No.	Name	No.	Name
50	JIMMY TALLMAN	57	CHUCK JOYNER	64	JERRY REINHOLT
51	JIMMY HUBBARD	58	CHET ROLLINS	66	DICK ROACH
53	JERRY HOLMAN	59	RUSS KONNEL, JR	90	JACK GORDON
54	STEVE GIMARELLI	60	STEVE KONNEL	94	STEVEN SMITH
55	DAN TUCKER	62	NORMAN HOLLARS	97	ROGER KORN
56	DICK DONACA	63	JERRY DOBBINS	111	DUKE HOOKER

What We Hated

      rain/ loose chains/ worn sprockets
      cars/ a muffled exhaust/ journalists
      bad gas/ oil leaks/ fouled plugs
      mud/ batteries/ cops/ curbs
      drivers who turned in front of you
      girls who wouldn't ride/lay
      Monday mornings

What We Loved

      Saturday mornings/ early/ sun
      clean bikes/ open exhausts
      tuned engines/ running cool
      a little alky in the tank
      cold beer/ hot coffee/ hot chicks
      open roads/ trails without rocks
      a good headlight/ riding buddies

On Seeing the Wild One

    Four of us downshifting/ four/ three/ two/ low
    exhausts backing off/ rumbling/ rolling throttles
    the line of faces outside the neighborhood theater
    turning toward our machines/ us/ the menace
    feet down/ rolling back wheels to the curb
    hit kill buttons/ pull compression releases
    in unison/ parked all in a neat row
    shucked off gloves/ stomped to the window in boots

    with popcorn there was a stupid love story
    then they came/ down the road/ Brando riding
    a Triumph/ trophy taped to the bars/ serious
    riding the wrong lane/ defying traffic
    riding a pretty square bike/ all road equipment
    a serious look on his puffy boyish face
    but riding the way we'd always wanted to
    not giving a damn/ we knew/ we knew

    and those other freaks/ Marvin's riding circus/ clowns
    what was their game?/ their future?/ stripped bikes
    dragging for beers/ riding right into the tavern
    who were they?

    Later/ swaggering out/ kicking it like Brando
    riding cool/ turning on down dark streets
    we knew they'd finally made a real bike film
    we knew we'd seen something

TIRED OF WAITING FOR PARTS"?

TIRED OF WAITING UNTIL THEY "COME FROM THE FACTORY"?

TIRED OF POOR SERVICE?

GET A

LEAVE IT TO YOUR **BSA**

 IS THE WORLD'S LARGEST MOTORCYCLE MANUFACTURER

HAS ONE OF THE FINEST DEALER SERVICE CHAINS BACKED BY HUGE SERVICE STOCKS ON BOTH COASTS.

Roy Burke
10-19-92

AMERICAN BRITISH CYCLES	ALLIED MOTORCYCLE SALES
5771 N. E. Union — Portland GA. 9188	3706 S. E. Powell Blvd. Portland 2, Oregon VE. 5405
Walt Ball Jack Warner	Roy Burke Hubert Simon

Dealers and Shops

Probably the oldest cycle shop in Portland was East Side Motorcycle Company at 525 NE Davis. Everything about the place was old, including the oil stained wooden floor. In the 1950s it was owned by Billy Ansenberger, who had raced cycles in the 1930s and 1940s. It was a long-time Harley-Davidson dealership, specializing in sales and service, and it always had a good supply of new and used motorcycles. East Side published a glossy newsletter called *Motorcycle News*, which was mailed to everyone with a current motorcycle license plate (the addresses were taken from DMV listing). It also published a *Used Motorcycle Bulletin* with a complete listing of current stock, sent by request. By the late 1950s East Side had also become a dealer for NSU motorcycles.

Johnny Payne's motorcycle shop was across the street from Washington High. Modified 1936 Ford roadster was owned by Bill Logus.

Probably the nicest cycle shop was Ray Gardener's shop at 2232 E. Burnside, which was then a new building. A few years earlier it had been located at 20th and S.E. Morrison, on the southwest corner, in what was also a new building. In the 1957 Portland phone book the East Burnside address was listed as Indian Northwest Sales Co. The Indian motorcycle company had gone out of business in 1953 but no doubt there was still a demand for parts and service as well as used cycles. Ray Gardner was also a dealer for AJS, Matchless and Zundapp motorcycles and all manner of Cushman scooters.

In 1954 a small car lot at N.E. 20th and Sandy bought a bunch of used motorcycles, and I have long thought that they came from Ray Gardner's shop, perhaps when it changed locations.

Allied Motorcycle Sales and Service was located at 3706 S.E. Powell Boulevard. It was owned by Roy Burke and Hubert Simon, both active racers. Burke won the Class C National Hill Climb on a Harley-Davidson and the Class

Dealers and Shops

A National Climb on an Indian. In 1955 he took top honors in the Big Bear Cross Country National Championship on a BSA.

Allied was a dealer for BSA, AJS, Matchless and Royal Enfield, and the showroom was always packed with new and used machines. Adjoining that was the parts department and beyond that was the repair area. Allied was always busy but the owners really raked in the bucks in the 1960s when the shop became the first dealer in Portland for Honda motorcycles.

Jack Warner and Walt "Fuzzy" Ball owned American-British Cycles. Rudy Rehbein built shop truck that won shows. This was years before Rancheros and El Caminos.

On the same street, at 50th and S.E. Powell, was Mort Becker's shop; It lacked a sign, but it was called Modern Motorcycles. The shop was non-descript: dark, narrow, oil stained floor, no wall art, no shiny new motorcycles. This place was a repair shop, not a dealership. You entered through the door facing Powell, walked along the single aisle between two rows of very used motorcycles until you came to the parts counter. To the right was another room, identical in size, long and narrow, which was where the repairs were made.

What the shop lacked in glitter it made up for in enthusiasm. Many a young biker spent his Saturdays here, maybe buying a part, maybe just talking. On various Sunday mornings, rain or shine, riders would gather in the parking lot of Bart's Drive-In (later called The Speck) across the street and would leave in a group, headed for Swan Island or The Old Homestead or wherever the run might be held that day. A kid I went to high school with, Gene Curry, got a job at the shop and became an excellent motorcycle mechanic and tuner, and a very competitive racer. The shop seemed to specialize in converting a rigid frame cycle into one with a swinging arm rear suspension by installing tubular shock absorbers from an automobile.

Doug Rambo had a cycle shop at 307 N.E. Broadway. Rambo had been an active motorcycle racer. His shop was called Western Motorcycle Co. It was a dealer for Triumph and Ariel motorcycles and Johnson Seahorse outboard motors. It was a distributor for Vincent, HRD, Velocette, Excelsior and Norton. By the mid-1950s it was a dealership for DKW automobiles. The shop was spacious, with light coming in the large windows facing Broadway and the western side street. It had a good display of cycles, and as a dealer/distributor for several makes it had many new cycles on the floor. I remember standing near the parts counter, looking at a large cork sheet covered with photographs of cycle riders, some from an earlier period.

Foster Sporting Goods was located at 80th and S.E. Harold. When it opened, just after WW II, it was called Foster Cycle and Sporting Goods Company, and soon billed itself as "The World's Largest Sports Supermarket". It was owned by Henning Helstrom; he wrote a book in 1961 called *The Oregon Sportsman's Guide* "the first of its kind". In the late 1940s, when cars were difficult to get because of the wartime shortage, Foster Sporting Goods had a large supply of new Servi-Cycles, a heavy-duty motorized bicycle. It also distributed the Blazer, a scooter designed for use by hunters and fishermen.

> MOTORCYLE rider. Honest and neat. 5-day week. Apply in person. 823 W Burnside.

Elden Wright (Takanori Okamoto collection)

Elden Wright

I go back a long way in the world of British motorcycles, mainly Triumphs, made in Coventry, England. The managing director of the Triumph corporation, Meridan Works, was Edward Turner. Edward Turner originally worked for Ariel motorcycles. He designed a square four Ariel. It had two 500cc engines that had two big square gears and the crankshafts turned in opposite directions. He took that design, half of it, and made a Triumph. With the Triumph, the pistons go up and down like a single cylinder, and they fire alternately.

The long and the short of this is that my cousins, this was before WW II, rode motorcycles, and I wanted to ride a motorcycle. But my dad wouldn't let me have a motorcycle because he said if you get one it'll kill you and that'll be the end of you! But I got one. On 3rd and NE Broadway there used to be a motorcycle store called Western Motorcycles. Doug Rambo owned the store and his brother Bob worked for him. Back in those days, if you bought a new motorcycle all you had to have was fire and theft insurance; the dealer didn't require any other insurance. They sold a motorcycle to a guy who lived in Pendelton, and he got to Arlington. In those days they had no air cleaner on these motorcycles, just kind of a bell intake on the carburetor. They had two kinds of magnetoes. One was a Lucas magneto, which had a hand operated advance and retard, like an old Model T Ford. Triumph came out with a BTH magneto, which had an automatic spark advance and retard. That was Triumph's new thing. Once in a while the retard and advance mechanism would get stuck in advance and when you went to start the thing up it would backfire, and the carburetor would catch on fire. The way you put the fire out in those old motorcycles--this was a 1948 model--was you just opened up the throttle a little farther and give it a big kick and it would suck the fire into the engine and start running again. Everybody who had one knew how to do that. They sold this new motorcycle to this guy who lived in Pendelton, he stopped in Arlington to buy gas, and he started it up and it backfired, they tried to put the fire out but couldn't so they dragged it out into the street. They called the fire department but by the time they got there the thing was burned up pretty good.

So they had that motorcycle in the back of the store at 3rd and Broadway. I bought a Mustang Colt, a small motorcycle, it had a British 125cc two-stroke engine in it. My dad let me buy it because it was not much more than a powered bicycle. They had this burned Triumph in the back of the shop--this was in 1949--and I kept looking at it and I said why don't you sell me that old piece of junk? They said no, no, you don't want to buy that thing, it's too burned. Finally I bought it, I overhauled it and I painted it and chromed the fender braces and did a lot of special work and when I got it all done I rode it down in front of the motorcycle shop and parked it. They said where did you get that motorcycle? It was painted fluorescent green, which in 1950 Ford came out with the only car that ever had a fluorescent paint.

Elden Wright

I rode that motorcycle with my buddy who bought a motorcycle and the two of us rode back to Indianapolis in 1950 to see the Indy 500 car race. Back in those days it was all two-lane road, no freeways. We made the trip, nobody got killed along the way!

I went to Vanport College back when it was in the flood area; it later became Portland State. Randy Francis went to school out there; he had a beautiful roadster. There were guys with Model As with Riley and Cragar heads. I used to go to the car races out on Union Avenue, that old 5/8ths of a mile dirt track. I saw Ray Chase win the 50 lap or 100 lap main event two years running with a 1941 Dodge coupe on a dirt track. There was a guy named Rajo Jack, a Black man, he had his race car out there but they got rained out. That was a race track, they made an amphitheater out there, they put a quarter-mile track on the inside. Shorty Templeman and Bob Gregg, they used to run midgets, V-860s and Offenhausers and Drakes—Harley 74 Drake engine. I was a race car enthusiast and I wanted to be a race car driver but I couldn't afford it so I ended up racing motorcycles instead.

After I fixed that burned up motorcycle, the guy I bought it from, Doug Rambo, said you ought to go to work for me, and I did. I was working on cars, I had a Model A roadster with a Chrysler six cylinder engine. I also did a lot of paint work. But I became a motorcycle mechanic. I worked for Rambo from 1952 until 1956. They also sold small cars. They sold a German-built little thing that I forget the name of, they had a 500cc twin engine and they were so light you could grab the rear bumper and lift the rear wheels off the ground. Then they became a dealer for DKW Automobiles.

Doug Rambo sold Nortons, Vincent Black Shadows, he sold a lot of Velocettes. During WW II the British used all their good materials to make war goods supplies, tanks and so on. The Velocettes, they had the camshafts that would wear out in 1,000 miles. They would flake off and go through the engine and ruin everything. A local guy, Pat Conolly, would use stellite and studite to make camshafts; that's hard material that never wears out. Well, Rambo ordered 50 Velocettes and they got them over here and they had pretty good luck selling them There was a glitch in the order. They called up the English and said where's our motorcycles? We ordered 50 and we haven't got them yet. So it ended up they got 100 of them. The first batch they got camshafts started wearing out and engines started disintegrating all over the place. Rambo got Pat Conolly to take the camshafts out of the brand new ones and weld them up with stellite and regrind them then they wouldn't ever wear out.

I was racing motorcycles in those days, and all of a sudden, the guy I was working for, Bob Rambo, he up and fired me for no reason. Somehow, somebody stole a motorcycle and took it all apart and sold the parts and somebody said it was me. He canned me on the spot. I went over to Roy Burke and Hubert Simon's store at 36th and Powell, Allied Motorcycles. They also used to sell televisions when TV first came out. I went to work for them.

Just after WW II they appointed an importer for Triumph motorcycles for the western part of the United States--Johnson Motors in Pasadena, California.

Ed Kretz was one of their salesmen, and Skip Fordyce in Riverside was another. The sales manager came through Portland calling on dealers and he called on the dealer who'd just canned me. I'd been working for Hubert and Roy for only a couple weeks. The dealer who canned me for no reason told the sales manager, I've made a terrible mistake. I canned one of the best guys I ever had working for me. The sales manager said maybe I better talk to him because I need a rep. So I had this Triumph experience and he took me out to dinner and the next morning we drove to Los Angeles and I went to work. That was 1956.

That was a terrific job, because I travelled all over. I used to go to England every year, because when they were making changes in the motorcycle they wanted the Americans to give their input, on paint, handlebars, tires, all that kind of stuff. Back in the days when Honda first came over here they jumped on Harley, they tried to sell those little bikes to Harley but Harley wouldn't have it. So they got on the Triumph group and started courting them. That's how the Honda thing really got started, they fed a bunch of our dealers. Then Triumph decided to make a three cylinder motorcycle. I went to England the last time, I took my wife with me because I was going to quit working for the British and started working for myself. I went to work for Bell helmets actually. I was in London, we walked across the London Bridge and I bought a pair of shoes. I put the shoes on and walked back across the bridge to the Hotel Commodore. Later the Americans bought London Bridge and moved it to Lake Havasu. I took that same pair of shoes and walked across London Bridge in Lake Havasu. I've got the only pair of shoes that have walked across that bridge in two continents!

Elden Wright in a promotional shot (Takanori Okamoto collection)

Al Drake on his 1951 BSA Gold Star at Indian Rock in 1955.

Choices

We make choices every day; sometimes we make them without knowing we're choosing. On the big things, such as good versus evil, the choice is usually obvious, and most of us would choose good. But there are those less obvious choices, subtle decisions, whose outcome may not be apparent until years later.

In 1955 the next door neighbor, Louis Marston, decided to put in a low retaining wall across the front of his property. Since he owned a double lot, he was faced with quite a job. But he had come from Italy and he was used to hard work. He had a huge garden, and grew tomatoes, peppers and garlic, which he used to make his own spaghetti sauce. In his extra lot he had put in an underground sprinkling system, which was a big deal in our lower class neighborhood. When he had finished his wall he talked my mother into extending the wall across the front of our single lot. Since he already had the forms built, all that needed to be done was a lot of shovel work, such as cutting away the incline between the street and our yard, and digging a ditch fifty feet long and a couple feet deep. Louis, who lived for hard work, assured us the he would help set the forms and pour the concrete. An added benefit was that the cement would be a base for a cyclone fence, which my mother considered a real asset to the property.

There was no question about who would do the work. I had all the time in the world. For two years I'd labored in a garage, but when the boss refused to give me a week off to go to Bonneville I made a big decision; I chose to quit my job and go to the speed trials. I have never regretted that choice. But now it was late August, I didn't have a job and there was no reason why I couldn't dig that ditch.

I was agreeable, more or less. It was simply that I was distracted by other things. If I had to choose between work or pleasure I chose pleasure. I worked occasionally at Ed's Richfield station, which gave me a few bucks for gas. It was late summer, and the weather was perfect for cruising. When I wasn't working I'd hang around the station, shooting the breeze with my friends. There was always someone to pal around with, and after dinner a couple of us would cruise 82nd, hoping to meet some girls who wanted to meet a couple guys. Things were more innocent in those days, and there was nothing evil implied if you started a conversation with a couple girls you didn't know. After some joking around, they'd just naturally get in the back seat and we'd drive to the top of Mt. Scott, to watch the sun set.

The business with the wall was perhaps a week's work, but I managed, through laziness and indolence, to stretch it on for three weeks. Louis would come over and check on the progress, encouraging me, even turning over a shovelful of dirt. One day he brought over a handful of smelt that he'd caught and smoked; I ate everything, including the heads and the roe. When he saw how

Choices

much I liked smoked smelt he promised a basketful of them when the job was done.

My mother was always on my back. She'd wake me early, urging me to get to work right after breakfast. I'd work for a couple hours, until the sun grew hot, then I'd take a break. My intentions were good, but between work and pleasure I chose the latter. I'd leave, intending to return in an hour and resume work, but that hour would stretch into several hours. In my defense, I have to say that during the end of the that summer, and until I took a job at Lee Cosart's, a Dodge-Plymouth dealer, the next month, I never felt so free. I was twenty, I had no bills, I lived at home and had no obligations. I owned a 1947 Ford mild custom, an A-V8 roadster and a BSA cycle, all paid for. I had friends, I knew a few girls and when I'd worked at Ed's Richfield I had a few bucks. In the evening I'd cruise around or go to a double feature at a neighborhood theater like the Aero or the Bob White. Perhaps I thought all of life would be like this.

One day when I should have been working on the wall I jumped on my BSA and took off. I was itchy, and I just wanted to go somewhere. The bike was a 30.50 Gold Star, silver tank, polished alloy engine, high pipe and it was spotless. The exhaust was stainless steel, with two feet of aluminum extension, which gave the exhaust a sharp rap on acceleration and a rich, loud rumble on deceleration. It was a joy to ride. I wore flat-bottom cycle boots, Levi's and a white T-shirt, clothes that made me feel free even as the wind tugged. I was darkly tanned from a week at Bonneville. I looked good and I felt good; there was no cloud on the horizon.

I rode the cycle to Blue Lake Park, about 15 miles east of Portland. The weather was great, the bike ran beautifully and there was no traffic. The park was on the north side of the lake and I was following the road that traversed the south side. Today that area has a thousand new houses, but fifty years ago it was largely open country, with impenetrable brush and groves of trees that ran right down to the water. Somehow in that deserted area I met a girl. Her parents owned a farm on the south side of the lake, a tall ramshackle house and a barn that had seen better days. I can't remember what they grew or whether they had any animals, just as I can't remember how I met her. I imagine we talked about stuff, the talk of young people, and at some point she took me to her house and introduced me to her mother. Later we walked to the edge of the lake. The day was blazing hot, but under the drooping willow trees there was a cool breeze. I'm sure it was her idea to go swimming; she probably did it every day. She took off her shoes and walked into the water until it came up to the pockets of her cut-off jeans. I kicked off my heavy cycle boots, shucked my T-shirt and Levis and walked into the water. I was not a great swimmer, but the water was seductively warm and it seemed to hold me up.

The next morning I made little pretense at working on the wall. By ten o'clock I was on my cycle and headed for Blue Lake Park. She was at the mail box, as if waiting for me. All that day and for the next week we lounged in the tall grass, then swam in the lake and returned to the grass. We talked, teased, almost touched. I can only imagine what we talked about, the stuff of youth, the unprofane ramblings of two people who were close, and could only get closer through language. It was the life projected in New Wave French movies. Years later I was at a rough campground near Aix-en-Provence, where young men and women, adolescents really, teased and argued and flirted, mouthing their cigarettes in a very sexual way, their cutoffs and bikinis ending at the point the imagination took over. That was the way it was at Blue Lake Park at the end of that summer, where wet clothing suggested much but everything was as innocent as the peanut butter sandwiches her mother made for us.

    I cannot remember how it ended. Perhaps the weather turned colder one day, or school started for the girl, or perhaps my mother delivered an ultimatum. I went back to work on the wall, and all the time I was digging I thought of her, not as a girl friend but a chum, a sidekick, someone I enjoyed being around. But I continued to dig, wider and deeper, determined to get the forms in the ground and the concrete poured before the first rains.

1951 BSA GOLDEN FLASH
$650.00
Never off the pavement. 1100 actual miles. Mould marks not even worn off the tires. Complete with pillion seat and pegs, Sportshield. This is a real buy for some lucky guy.
Send 10c for snapshot of this chrome and black beauty. **Write or call PAT RUSSELL at 229 Woodruff Avenue, Arcadia, California**

Choices

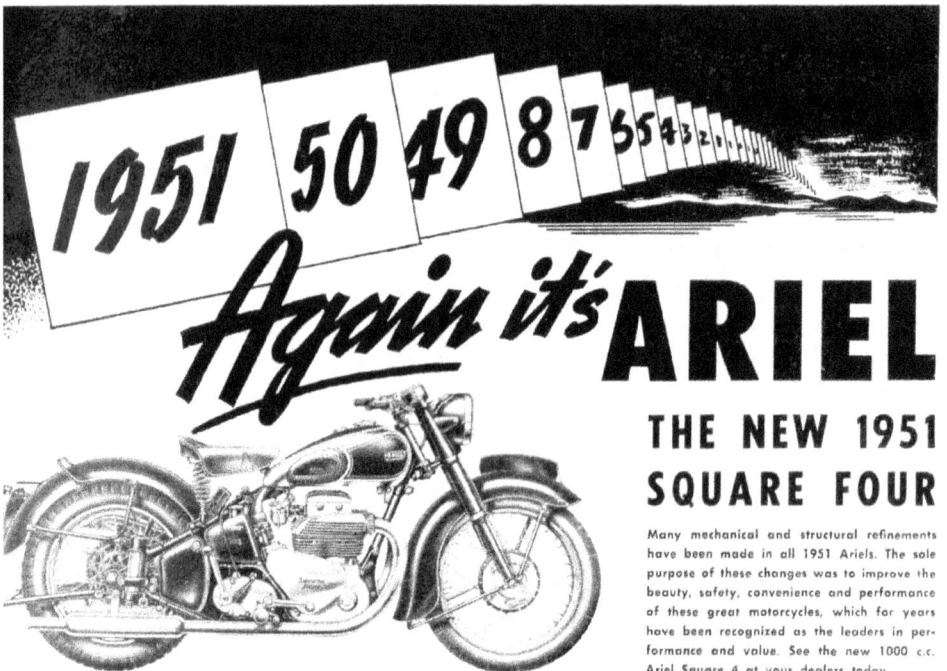

1951 RED HUNTER TWIN—500 c.c.

Principal change is a new flywheel assembly with a weight increase of about 20%, resulting in a smoother engine and transmission, without affecting acceleration.

1951 RED HUNTER SINGLE—500 c.c.

The most important change in this model is the new cam gear, which dispenses with two separate cams by employing a single cam of double width.

Rear wheel removal is simplified by the manner in which the mud guard pivots forward.

New tank is free of instrument panel, filler cap is centered, and capacity increased by ¼ of a gallon.

ARIEL ARE THE ONLY BRITISH MANUFACTURERS OFFERING YOU THE WIDE CHOICE OF FOUR, TWIN & SINGLE CYLINDER 1951 MODELS.

A drag bike with two Triumph engines

Cut Downs

My mind is getting so cloudy that there are times when I cannot remember crucial details from the past. What, for example, did we call those much modified British street bikes of the 1950s? Were they called "scoots?" That name might confuse them with scooters, which they were not. They were certainly not called "fat bobs," a term reserved for modified Harleys. Nor were they called "café racers", which they most resembled, but that term hadn't gained currency in the 1950s. I'm calling them "cut downs", a term which might have existed back then.

Actually, there weren't so many such cycles on the street, not enough to form a sub-genre. In memory the whole subject diminishes to one guy, a guy whose name perhaps I never knew, who built at least three of these bikes. Two were "poppers", single cylinder bikes, and one was a twin. It was not uncommon to see a bike with a small gas tank but this guy went way beyond that. He took a bike, a 19" Velocette, and stripped it of front and rear fenders, horn, pillion seat, chain guard and anything else that could be removed. He painted the frame black, and used a small gas tank from a BSA Bantam, which he painted white. He narrowed the seat, and replaced the stock headlight and taillight with small units; he got rid of the battery and wired the lights to the magneto. He had the oil tank chrome plated. All the aluminum pieces on the engine—crankcase, pushrod towers, etc.–were highly polished until that engine looked like a jewel. The spark plug wire was red, as was the neoprene fuel line. For handlebars he used J bars, which curved upward, giving that lightweight cycle the appearance of a delicate insect.

He had two singles that were rebuilt in that manner, the Velocette and a Royal Enfield, or an Ariel, or perhaps a Matchless, I can't be certain, and he had a twin, a Triumph from the late 1940s. It was similar to the singles, having been stripped of all road equipment, but the aluminum parts had been polished and metal turned giving the bike a no-nonsense appearance; it looked precise, surgical, a piece of rocket science. The twin exhausts, chromed, swept backward and slightly upward, ending in a pair of megaphones.

I don't recall that anyone followed his lead; his interest never became a trend. Whichever bike the guy chose to ride, he sat upright, hands resting lightly on the grips, head turned slightly, as if he were looking at the far curb, and he rode slowly, perhaps five miles under the speed limit, as if showing the bike off. Come to think of it, maybe we called his bikes "putt putts."

Hauling bikes to Long Beach Gypsy Run in September, 1954.

Getting Home

I can't remember all the details of this story, but as I recall the event it seems both typical of those days and yet odd enough to write down. I do know that it happened on a beautiful spring day in 1955 because I decided to ride my BSA Gold Star to work. Somewhere along the line the rod that went through the multiple clutches broke, and I was without a clutch. This had happened once before, on the first day I rode the bike. The BSA was so beautiful and I was so happy. Everything was tight and new. I cruised through my neighborhood, enjoying the sound of the exhaust, in no hurry to be anywhere. Through low gear, through second gear, and when I went for third—there was nothing! The clutch lever went limp! I kicked it up into second without a clutch, made a U-turn and headed for home. I'd ridden my cycle only a few blocks!

On this day I made it to work in the same manner, keeping it moving, shifting without a clutch, and when I got to work I parked it. All morning I wondered how I would get the bike back home. At noon, as I recall, I walked to the car lot two blocks away, the place where I bought my first cycle, probably to ask advice. I knew I'd have to take it to the cycle shop, as I'd done before, but first I just wanted to get it home. The lot boy was John Farlow, a guy I'd gone to Franklin High with, and who I rode with on the cycle trails. He later developed into a good cycle mechanic and a fast rider, who eventually earned a national number.

I don't know the circumstances of John's current bike but it didn't have any lights. Maybe he had just got it, and, like me, he just wanted to ride it home. Anyway, putting our minds together, we saw a possibility that could solve our problem. After work I pushed my BSA two blocks to the lot where John worked and we stood around and talked for a half hour. In those days traffic was nothing like it is today, and in the half hour we killed the evening rush was just about over. We stood on the corner and watched the five o' clock traffic rush diminish to a piddle. But by six o' clock the sky had grown dark.

Our plan was simple. John didn't have any lights on his bike, so he would follow close behind, letting me lead the way. I didn't have a clutch so I couldn't easily stop for every light or stop sign. Fortunately, there were far fewer of both in those days, so once I got going I hoped I could keep going. John promised to get me through those stops.

Sometimes we rode down main streets, but whenever possible we took side streets. We rode south on 20th, me leading, lights on, John close behind. I could see the stop lights at Burnside so I slowed down in order to hit them when green. The same thing at Hawthorne. Then we got on side streets as we moved toward Powell. If there was a stop sign or a light John would race past me, stop at the intersection, raise his hand if cars were coming or wave me on if there was no traffic. I trusted him completely. I cranked it on, shot past John and through the intersection, then slowed until John caught up. We did this for miles, through many intersections, and I never had to stop. Today I-205 cuts across southeast

Getting Home

Portland, limiting east-west access to a few main streets, but in those days there was no freeway and there were a hundred side streets that allowed through traffic. So for perhaps ten miles we progressed in this manner, John racing past me to check on traffic, me racing through intersections without stopping, riding in a totally illegal manner. When I got to 92nd I waved John off, knowing I could make it home from there, but John, who lived about a mile away, continued to follow. That was the kind of guy he was. That was the way bikers were, happy to help another guy on a bike.

Glenn Wright pulled his and cousin Art Luft's cycles behind Glenn's 1940 Ford tudor.

1951 ANNUAL
25 Mile Pacific Coast Championship Motorcycle Race

PORTLAND MEADOWS RACE COURSE
PORTLAND, OREGON

PRESENTED BY WILLIAM P. KYNE AND ARD PRATT

Officials

TOM BODEN	A. M. A. Referee
PAT VIDAN	Starter
JOHN MARTINOLICH	Pit Steward
JIM SYNDER	Asst. Pit Steward
ROSS LANGLITZ	Pit Gate Clerk
JIM FOSS	Asst. Pit Gate Clerk
RAY E. GARNER	Announcer
NICK NICHOLS	Timer
TOM BODEN	Timer Judge
STAN NESS	Track Flagman
ADA KOCHS	Head Checker
CHARLES MILLER	Technical Committee
BILL TATERSALL	Technical Committee
BUD DAVIS	Technical Committee
RAY GARNER	Competition Committee

Departments and Committees

ROSE CITY MOTORCYCLE CLUB	Usherettes
SHERIFF'S AERO SQUADRON	Parking
DISPLAYS	George Schantin
DISPLAYS	Roy Burke
DISPLAYS	Bob Rambo
DISPLAYS	Jack Warner
DISPLAYS	Ray Garner

The Flags and What They Mean

WHITE FLAG	START OF RACE
YELLOW FLAG	ONE MORE LAP TO GO
WHITE WITH BLACK CENTER	PULL OVER RIDER PASSING
CHECKERED FLAG	FINISH OF RACE
RED FLAG	INDICATES DANGER ON COURSE
BLACK FLAG	DISQUALIFICATION

SPORT HARLEY POLICE

Parts — Oil — Service — Accessories

AMATEURS

No.	Name	Bike	City	TIME
2Y	CHADWICK, RALPH	HARLEY-DAVIDSON	SAN LORENZO, CALIF.	
28Y	BORING, MARION	HARLEY-DAVIDSON	VALLEJO, CALIF.	
32W	BOORE, RALPH	HARLEY-DAVIDSON	BEND, OREGON	
49W	CRANE, FRANK	HARLEY-DAVIDSON	ESTACADA, ORE.	
52W	BARON, CHICK	TRIUMPH	GREAT FALLS, MONT.	
54Y	BALL, HAROLD	HARLEY-DAVIDSON	PORTLAND, OREGON	
55Q	DAY, HUB JR.	TRIUMPH	REDMOND, OREGON	
59W	SERGEANT, HAROLD	TRIUMPH	CORVALLIS, OREGON	
62W	ANSENBERGER, BILLY	INDIAN	PORTLAND, OREGON	
68W	JONES, KEN "CASEY"	HARLEY-DAVIDSON	SPRINGFIELD, ORE.	
74Y	FLOURNEY, WALTER	HARLEY-DAVIDSON	REDWOOD CITY, CAL.	
77W	MAJHORS, CLIFF	HARLEY-DAVIDSON	PORTLAND, OREGON	
77Y	SIMPSON, CAL	INDIAN	LAKEVIEW, OREGON	
80W	WINTERS, VERN	B.S.A.	PORTLAND, OREGON	
81Y	MASTERSON, CHUCK	B.S.A.	REDWOOD CITY, CAL.	
86Q	KELLOGG, DICK	HARLEY-DAVIDSON	PORTLAND, OREGON	
92Y	HUBBARD, GRANT	HARLEY-DAVIDSON	OAKLAND, CALIF.	
93R	NUNES, BOBBY	HARLEY-DAVIDSON	ARROYO GRANDE, CAL.	
99W	BLOOMQUIST, JACK	HARLEY-DAVIDSON	TACOMA, WASH.	
53N	GUNTER, ALBERT	TRIUMPH	OAKLAND, CAL.	
73Q	MILLER, DICK	INDIAN	TACOMA, WASH.	
89Y	McAFEE, HUGH	TRIUMPH	MENLO PARK, CAL.	

NOVICES

No.	Name	Bike	City	TIME
4Q	HALE, WALT	HARLEY-DAVIDSON	WALLA WALLA, WASH.	
23W	McCOY, JACK	B.S.A.	BURBANK, CALIF.	
37Q	DONAHOE, DAN	HARLEY-DEVIDSON	MEDFORD, OREGON	
42W	PHELPS, DOUGLAS	INDIAN	TACOMA, WASH.	
49Q	KERN, ROBERT	B.S.A.	PORTLAND, OREGON	
54Q	SCHERRER, GENE	VELOCETTE	THE DALLES, OREGON	
64Q	HERSCHBACH, GEORGE	INDIAN	SALEM, OREGON	
72W	WALL, JOHN	HARLEY-DAVIDSON	WINLOCK, WASH.	
73W	HARRIS, ROBERT	HARLEY-DAVIDSON	TACOMA, WASH.	
75W	TINDALL, RON	TRIUMPH	PORTLAND, OREGON	
76W	LEE, DONALD	VELOCETTE	ASTORIA, OREGON	
82W	DAILY, BOB	HARLEY-DAVIDSON	MEDFORD, OREGON	
91W	BLAIR, NORMAN	B.S.A.	PORTLAND, OREGON	
96Q	FORRESTER, EDWARD	B.S.A.	SALEM, OREGON	

COMMERCIAL DELIVERY
DAVIDSON
Everything For The Motorcycle Rider

EXPERTS

No.	Name	Bike	City	TIME
7Y	COOPER, GEORGE	HARLEY-DAVIDSON	VALLEJO, CALIF.	
10W	PUGH, VERN	HARLEY-DAVIDSON	PUYALLUP, WASH.	
17W	AIKINS, LENNY	HARLEY-DAVIDSON	PUYALLUP, WASH.	
31Y	WEST, CHARLES	HARLEY-DAVIDSON	SAN JOSE, CALIF.	
60	WALTERMIRE, BBILL	HARLEY-DAVIDSON	COLUMBUS, OHIO	
62	EARWELL, C. A. "RED"	HARLEY-DAVIDSON	TACOMA, WASH.	
64W	GARBER, JIM	B. S. A.	PORTLAND, OREGON	
69	RICE, B. W. "RED"	EXCELSIOR	PORTLAND, OREGON	
70	THIESSEN, EUGENE	B. S. A.	EUGENE, OREGON	
75Q	WOOD, HARLYN	HARLEY-DAVIDSON	BOISE, IDAHO	
82Q	TINDALL, DONALD	TRIUMPH	PORTLAND, OREGON	
84X	BRUNGADE, BERT	TRIUMPH	LOS ANGELES, CALIF.	
85Y	FAGUNDES, ED.	HARLEY-DAVIDSON	VALLEJO, CALIF.	
94Y	ALCALA, GEORGE	HARLEY-DAVIDSON	OAKLAND, CAL.	
95Y	SLACK, BOB	TRIUMPH	GREAT FALLS, MONT.	

Red Rice

NOVICES -- Continued

No.	Name	Bike	City
102W	WILHOUR, JACK	HARLEY-DAVIDSON	SEATTLE, WASH.
104W	RIDGEWAY, BILL	B. S. A.	PORTLAND, OREGON
116W	BAISLEY, WES	HARLEY-DAVIDSON	MADRAS, OREGON
123Q	PURCELL, DAVE	NORTON	SHERWOOD, OREGON
125Q	JORDAN, RODNEY	B. S. A.	OREGON CITY, ORE.
128W	HARLAND, PAUL	B. S. A.	PORTLAND, OREGON
128Y	WILHITE, DONALD	TRIUMPH	MODESTO, CALIF.
136Q	GRANES, RUSSELL	B. S. A.	OREGON CITY, OREGON
157W	SIGGSTEDT, ONE	B. S. A.	PORT ANGELES, WASH.
161W	ZUMWALT, DEL	HARLEY-DAVIDSON	SEATTLE, WASH.
177W	WATSON, BOB	INDIAN	SALEM, OREGON
180Y	BUCHMILLER, HENRY JR.	TRIUMPH	LODI, CALIF.
	McDONALD, KENNY	HARLEY-DAVIDSON	WINLOCK, WASH.
11Q	O'NEAL, LYLE	B. S. A.	TACOMA, WASH.
56Q	WRIGHT, WAYNE	NORTON	TACOMA, WASH.

A three wheel Harley-Davidson motorcycle with custom built commercial side hack.

Three-Wheeling

From 1937 until 1963 Harley-Davison made a three wheel motorcycle. Called a Servi-Cycle, it was mostly used by car dealers or service stations to pick up and deliver cars. A customer would call with a car problem or a car that needed periodic service, and the shop would send a man, usually the lot boy, to the person's house on the Servi-Cycle. He'd hook the Servi-Cycle to the back bumper of the car and drive the car to the dealership. It was a neat way to handle a customer's request, back in the days when service mattered.

My friend Phil Gamelgard remembers when his next-door neighbor rode a three wheel Servi-Cycle, because the man occasionally rode it home at lunch time. "He worked for Smith-Lyons Packard on Grand Avenue (in Portland, Oregon). He said they were the most dangerous damn thing, you get up to about 40 mph and that thing would start shaking!"

Phil also knew the man who rode the Servi-Cycle for Frank's Chevrolet. "Frank's was the last dealership to have those Servi-Cycles (in the 1960s). They had two or three of them. This guy, Dick O'Neil, was a real character. He was a pretty heavy drinker for one thing. Seems like he was always hung over when I saw him. But he had varied abilities. Jack Dickey told me that he went to the Star (a burlesque theater) one night and here was Dick O'Neil doing the warm-up act. He was a funny-looking guy and here he was the stand-up comedian.

"Jack Dickey worked at Fields Chevrolet and one day he saw Dick O'Neil crossing Union Avenue, walking as if he were terribly crippled, moving very slowly, holding up traffic. When he got to the middle he looked at all the traffic that had backed up and suddenly he began to run into the store. You never knew what he was going to do next!

"When I was a kid, 18 years old, I worked for an ambulance company and Dick O'Neil was a driver. He knew Portland like the back of his hand. But he was a hard drinker. He came to work one day and he was so hung over he couldn't hold his head up. One time he went down Hawthorne in a '50 Cad ambulance and he came to the bottom of the hill and he said he had to slow way down to 76 mph. He drove a three-wheeler the same way!

"Some traffic cops also had three-wheelers; they'd drive along slowly and they had a long stick with a piece of chalk on the end, they'd make a mark on a tire and come back in an hour; if the car hadn't moved they'd give the guy a ticket. When I worked at Francis Ford I remember the switchboard operator, Patty Kern, she used to say 'Officer Billings is now marking the cars!' Francis had loudspeakers outside the building as well as inside. She'd broadcast all around the whole frigging neighborhood and guys would come running from everywhere to move their cars!"

Three-Wheeling

Mark Budlong remembers his experiences with three wheelers: "When I worked at Billingsly Pontiac I was the parts pickup and delivery boy. I normally drove a little Chevy pickup, but one day they were working on it and they needed some item picked up, and so I took the Harley Servi-Cycle. I went across the Hawthorne Bridge, on that grating, and oh shit, I thought I was going to crash for sure. I went back and forth, back and forth on that steel grating. I'm not sure I'd ride a motorcycle across that bridge today.

Most dealerships and shops had 3 wheel Servi-cycles to pick up and deliver customers' cars.

"I'm over at Allied Motorcycle one day and Roy Burke had to go downtown to get something. He had this Harley with a sidecar, and the sidecar was for carrying stuff—it was long enough to haul a motorcycle on it. He said, hey Mark, you want to go? And I said all right. He said get in the box. I did, and I had to sit with my back toward the front; I was riding backward. Jesus Christ, what a ride! Because he could ride a motorcycle like nobody you ever saw. I'm sitting backward looking up—all I could see was the sky. Half the time the sidecar wheel was off the ground. What a ride that was!"

In 1955 I got a job at Lee Cosart's Dodge-Plymouth dealership. It had an old Servi-Cycle that I believe had a 45 cubic inch motor; maybe it was a 61 incher, but it did not have that much power. Since no one rode it I used to take it out whenever I could, such as a quick trip over to my bank, the Benjamin Franklin at 39th and SE Hawthorne, on my lunch hour. Because I was not going to school or learning much on the job, I figured driving or riding different vehicles was part of my education. I rode that thing as fast as it would go. One thing I liked to do was to go around a city corner and lean it over as far as I could. That'd bring the outside rear wheel off the ground and when it was in the air I'd crank on the gas; when the wheel came down it'd lay a little rubber!

Riding Bike in the Fifties

No one every complained about me riding the cycle; they probably assumed I was on a parts run. One day we had a couple inches of snow and I took the three-wheeler out. I was going up a slight grade on SE Davis, a side street, and I began to turn the handlebars to the left, then the right, applying the gas; the rear of the cycle swung one way, then the other. I was always able to correct the slide until I got going a little too fast and the rear end swung to the right, hit a parked car and bounced off. I let up on the gas and rode slowly back to the dealership and parked the cycle, hoping that no one had seen me.

The only time someone complained was when I took the cycle and I should have taken the truck. I'd get down to Central Motor Parts, the MoPar warehouse under the Grand Avenue overpass, and when I called in I was told to bring a fender for a '53 Dodge or three 1955 Plymouth bumpers, a load too big to fit in the cycle. I'd have to drive the length of Grand Avenue and get the truck and go back. Then someone would complain!

It wasn't until I'd left Lee Cosart and moved on to another job, one that lacked a three-wheeler, that I was told how dangerous they were. They apparently have a tendency to flip over at speed on an uneven road, when the box lifts up and goes over the handlebars! That could have been the end of my education!

Jerry Taylor (left) owned this '32 3-window with new Chrysler V-8. The other guy owned the chromed bike. Both members of the Montavilla Four Stroke club.

Impressions

Bill Langley was a perpetual biker who claimed to know every biker in Portland:

"That BSA I bought at Jack Warner's shop in 1952, a professor at Reed College pulled out in front of me on Woodstock and I went right into the car. Broke my right leg, a compound fracture, it was a year and a half before I could walk. I came within inches of losing that leg. I was just a kid then, 23 or so.

"We'd go to the Gypsy Tour (at Long Beach) and we'd get in races on the sand and I'd be half-bagged, fall off, bust something up. Every year I'd go there. If I rode down I'd come back in a car, something in a cast, or using crutches, some damn thing."

Phil Gamelgard grew up in Montavilla, and as a kid he loved to stand around and watch a group of bikers who hung out near his house. "There was a motorcycle club in Montavilla called the Four Strokers. Some members were Jerry Campbell, Jerry Taylor, Don Backstrand and others. All had modified British cycles. They even had a club house at 68th and SE Glisan. I can still remember them pulling up to the club house. I thought it was so cool, all those bikes. The guys wore black leather jackets, black engineer boots with the wedge soles, little black caps, black leather gloves, they had their Levis cut to the right length. It was all too neat.

"They even had an airplane inside the clubhouse with the wings removed. It was a Piper Cub or something. It probably belonged to Jerry Taylor; I don't know how he got it in there. He also had that '32 3-window with the Chrysler V-8—he bought that engine new at Central Motor Parts. I'd never seen anything like that car."

Mike Miller is a car guy who also owned several cycles; his experiences date from the late 1950s: "The races at Sidewinders drew big crowds; there were a lot more people than there were seats usually. A lot of people would stand up between the bleachers. I'd say that the average attendance was 1,500 people.

"There were many accidents, but not too often was someone taken away in an ambulance. I remember Gary Davis busted his ankle all to hell there one night; he was in a cast for six months.

"(Keith) Preskey gave them a helluva ride out there. Gary Davis won often. Sliding John Farlow won many times. Sonny Burres won quite a few.

"Clancy Langman was the starter and I remember one time he dropped the flag so low he fell over the starting gate; I know that happened many times. He was a longshoreman—I worked with him on the docks and he was always stealing shit. I know that one night he stole about 30 bicycles. He asked if I wanted to be his lookout and I said, Clancy, I'm not going to say a word, I'm

Impressions

just leaving. I don't know how he never got caught. His house was packed with stolen stuff. I told him he was going to get killed taking stuff home and one night he got hit by burglars and they shot him dead. It'd take a semi-truck to unload that house.

"The cops were always drunk at Sidewinders. The Clackamas County Sheriffs who were hired as security. Their shirts would be unbuttoned, beer stains all over them. It was the only place I've actually seen cops drunk."

Bob Classen bought and sold many motorcycles during the 1950s, and he remembered a couple of them recently: "The first one was a BSA I bought in 1954. I bought it from a friend of my older brother. I think I paid $175—a lot of money for a high school kid. My folks said, well you can't ride it to school in your junior year but you can ride it in your senior year. But by then I'd had a dozen motorcycles. I had a nice 500cc single with the springer rear end. It was heavier, it wouldn't have been good for track racing but it was more comfortable on the road and it had a fatter seat. The rear wheel had only about an inch or two of travel, but it was better than a rigid! The few BSAs that were in the neighborhood were all rigids. Actually, I had a couple springers. One I had apart and ended up putting a Ford piston in it and it ran great.

John Farlow, 31W and Andy Anderson, 24 come around the turn..

"One I had was really fast. It had a big Amal carburetor on it. I took that big carb off and traded it at Allied, at 37th and Powell, for a stock carb. God it was fast! That thing just ran like anything. The others were okay but that particular one was something else. A friend got a brand new BSA twin, which had a lot more horsepower than mine, and I could just kill his bike up to about 70 mph. I must've been five bike lengths ahead of him and then that twin—zoom!—he'd get by me like I was standing still!"

Fighting it out for the lead are John Farlow, 31W, Clark Gable 16Q, Vern Perry, 17W and Bill Partlow, 20Q.

Glenn Wright was a biker in the 1950s; his brother, Elden Wright, was the west coast representative for Triumph. I asked Glenn about those early Gypsy Tours.

"I went every year. It was fantastic. We stayed at some motel in Long Beach. We'd usually go beach sliding the next day, me and Art Luft. A bunch of guys going in a big circle, going nuts.

"Some years they had races. Kind of like a Daytona thing, through the dirty old rough sand and then down to the smooth sand along the water. Some of those guys would go 70, 80 mph. It depended on how big the course was. There were accidents—I saw a guy get his leg busted one day.

"They used to have a big parade down the main drag the first evening. The clubs would all ride together, some would have a pole on the bike with a club flag on it. The cops didn't bother us. Most of the guys behaved themselves. The merchants liked us because we brought money to the town."

Impressions

Bikers gathering in downtown Long Beach, Washington for the Gypsy Tour.

Riding Bike in the Fifties

Chuck Classen slidin' on beach

Dick Weber (left), Bob Classen (right),
Long Beach, Washington Gypsy Tour

Mark Budlong on his BSA. His father, Howard Budlong, owned Bill's Steak House in Parkrose, where racers hung out.

Mark Budlong

We lived on 27th and Klickitat. My folks bought the house, it was the first house they ever owned. They bought it in December, 1941 and we moved from a rental house over on N. Commercial, right across from Jefferson High School. We made the move in a garbage truck!

Actually, we didn't move a lot of stuff. My dad went all out. He bought that house, and he redecorated it inside, and he bought a new stove and refrigerator, new furniture, almost everything was new.

One neighbor kid, his father was the parts manager at Billingsly Pontiac; his dad helped him build a sidewalk car. It had a one cylinder gasoline engine. The car looked like a Jeep. Then another kid, Joe Nudelman, built one. Then when I moved into the neighborhood I said I have to have one of those, so I built one. I built a couple, in fact. The hardest problems we had were steering and brakes. We actually got spindles, and we used pneumatic tires. Most of the guys used cables for steering, and that was a pain because the cables kept stretching. I used an automotive wheel and shaft and drilled a hole into the tie rod, and the only problem then was that you could only turn the wheel about an inch either way.

Then I got a scooter—a brand new Cushman Heavy Duty motor scooter, it had a little trunk on it, and a nice windshield on it, and a two speed transmission. It ran great. Hardly any maintenance. I got my first ticket with that. We were out on Marine Drive and a county sheriff came along and stopped to talk with us. He asked whose scooter it was and I said it's mine. He said, you don't have a driver's license and I said no. I was only 14. So he gave me a ticket, but he let me ride it home! The judge told my dad, well you can't let that kid ride and later my dad said, bullshit, go ahead and ride. I never did get another ticket. What bothered me about that Cushman was that it would only go about 35 mph, and at the same time there was another scooter (Mustang?), it had a Ford piston, that darn thing would go 70 mph. Actually, I don't like scooters; I think they're the most dangerous thing known to man. The wheels are too small, so there's no natural stability to them. You can ride a bicycle with your hands off the handlebars, you can ride a motorcycle with your hands off the handlebars. But try that with a scooter! You'll go right on your noggin.

Then I got a car, a '36 Ford 3-window, I bought it in the dark, because my parents said I could, and it was a hunk of crap! I took it out to Al Reamer's shop, and Al said that the frame was broken. I swapped it for a '31 Model A roadster with a Ford V-8 engine.

There was a young kid who lived behind Arndt brothers' service station; his name was Ed Bierly. He went to Grant with me, he was a nice kid, he had a Triumph Trophy model. He knew that I wanted a motorcycle, and there was an unemployed brick layer with a broken leg – and this was in December, there was a little snow on the ground – and he had a 1940 Triumph Speed Twin that had a tubular front end on it—they normally didn't, but it was all in pieces. Several boxes of parts. I bought it from the brick layer, he really needed the money, and we took it to two brothers—one worked for the phone company and the other was a mechanic—Mort Becker! He put the motorcycle all together for me! I can't remember what I did with it – obviously I sold it somewhere.

Mark Budlong on his new BSA Golden Flash, a 40" twin. He was in the Navy, sold the bike in Japan.

My next bike was a Triumph Tiger. It was beautiful, it was silver and black. I bought it used but this bike was perfect—there wasn't a scratch on it. I thought about stripping it all down, like Cliff Mahjors used to do, but instead I traded it to Allied Motorcycles. They just grabbed it. My next bike was a new BSA Gold Star. One day the price was $1000, and then they devalued the pound and the next day a new Gold Star was $795. They came with a great big TT carburetor, and those bastards were the hardest things to start. I changed that carburetor on mine. I put a low straight pipe with a snuffer on it, and that gas tank, which was mostly chrome with a little paint, I had the painted part done in black. Then I got a Gold Star sticker and put it on. It really looked good. I wanted it to look like a flat track bike—I still like that look. On my Harley (today) I have to have staggered duals, like the old WRH Harley.

Of the Montavilla bunch, Don Backstrand was the nicest guy over there, he was a machinist. Don is the guy who showed me what to do with my Gold Star. I had to put risers on the handlebars, to raise them up. I had to do that because Don Tindall did that on his Triumph. Don Backstrand told me have the seat narrowed and have Ross Langlitz recover your seat and then make a nice little pillion, you don't want a big 4" high pillion, you want about an inch and a half or 2" pillion.

Eddie Bierly and I went to University of Portland with our motorcycles. Rain or shine. We had little lap aprons, Ross Langlitz made them for us. We folded them up and held them behind the pillion pad with rubber bands if it wasn't raining.

One year I took my Gold Star on the Gypsy Tour to Long Beach, Washington. That was where Dick Arndt got killed after WW II. I was standing there talking to Roy Burke and somebody screamed. I turned around and there was a motorcycle probably 25 feet in the air. What had happened was that Dick Arndt, who was, of the Arndt brothers, the youngest boy, Elmer was the oldest, Lester was his younger brother, another brother and they had a sister too. Dick came up from California on a Harley, he took me for a ride on it and scared the crap out of me. He started racing an Indian for Ray Gardner, and that was the new Indian, the Warrior, that looked like a Triumph. He did pretty damn good! Basically, he was a gutty sonofagun. Anyway, we decided to go on the Gypsy tour, and I took his motorcycle and my Gold Star to Long Beach on a trailer, pulled by my '49 Ford, almost a new car. Dick and some other guys had made a kind of TT course on the beach and they were racing around it. Three guys from Vancouver—I think they were the Vancouver Black Cats—they were drunker than hell, they came screaming down the beach and two of them hit Dick. One guy busted his knee, another guy it killed him and it killed Dick. That was the only Gypsy Tour I ever went to—it must have been 1949.

Elmer Arndt promoted both national motorcycle races at Portland Meadows. And that gave me carte blanche to go anywhere I wanted at Portland Meadows—they said if you're a friend of Elmer Arndt you must be all right.

I rode that Gold Star to California when I went in the Navy. I was stationed near San Francisco but I rode it down to Los Angeles. We went everywhere, went to the bike races at Carrell Speedway, saw some of the best motorcycle racing I've ever seen in my life, just tremendous racing. It was about a half mile track, with a 2" cushion, so they'd cross it up in the corners just like a speedway bike. We went to the Milne brothers' shop, they were famous racers. In the course of riding around I took off that TT carburetor and put a regular carburetor on it, which made it easier to ride.

You could store your motorcycle in San Francisco at the Harley dealer, that was Dudley Perkins in downtown San Francisco. You could store it upstairs and they charged very little. This was in the middle of winter and I was going to go home on leave (to Portland, Oregon) and I read the weather reports, it was raining in San Francisco, in the Siskiyou Mountains. I went upstairs at Dudley Perkins and I started that bike up and it sounded terrible, sounded like it would hardly run.

I decided that I wasn't going to ride that BSA so I got on a bus and went home, back to Portland, and BSA had come out with the new Golden Flash, a 40

Motorcycling Families! Above, Don and Ron Tindall on their 1955 KHRM's flank their Dad, "Slick" Tindall on his 1955 74 OHV Model FLHF. (Photo by Earl Cohen). Below, Ella Mikkalo and Naadene Clark, motorcycling sisters from The Dalles shown on their 74 OHV's, and on the right is Jack Rutis of Portland with his 1955 165. Jack's buddy, Bob Ross, just ordered a new 165 for himself, so they'll really be having fun together.

inch twin, with suspension in the rear—my Gold Star was a rigid. I said gee I wish I had my bike here to trade it in. Well, old Roy Burke was pretty sharp; he called down to Dudley Perkins and they crated it up and sent it up to Portland. I'm standing at Allied Motorcycles and the bike arrived, almost overnight. They unloaded it at Allied Motorcycles and Burke rode it out of the crate, gave it a kick and it started right up and it sounded beautiful! Anyway, I traded it in on a brand new Golden Flash. It wasn't very racy looking, but it was a helluva better road bike.

I never broke a bone. I crashed, I should've killed myself. We had been at a Division picnic off the ship up above Santa Clara; California, up in the mountains. We'd been drinking beer all day and playing softball. We came down the mountain on an asphalt two-lane road, when we crashed. I had a friend of mine behind me, Cranston Devill, there was a bank beside me on the right hand side with about a two foot shoulder. We came around a left hand corner and here was this boulder sitting right in the road. I knew I wasn't going to make the corner. I thought, well, I could drop it and hit it with the bottom of the bike or I could hit it square. I hit it square, and it launched both of us, me to the middle of the road, him to the shoulder, and the bike did a flip in the air, shoved the front wheel under the engine and it came down on the rear wheel. We both had little cuts on our heads, and I had a terrible road rash on my left leg. But nothing broken. But we fixed that bike because there was a dealer in that little town of Port Whyneemi, he was a Triumph dealer, he was a helluva nice guy, he let me do anything, I don't know why he did. We took that bike all apart and sent the frame to LA and they straightened it and we put it all back together and it ran fine.

I took that bike to Japan and sold it over there. I was able to take that bike on the ship because we had a real good captain. And because I was in electronics repair division; there were only about six of us in the repair division and three of us had motorcycles. I took my BSA and another kid had a BSA, and this other kid from Alabama, a real smart kid, he had a Vincent Black Shadow of all things. We took them all to Japan. We had a hard time getting them on the base to get to the ship, we had to have special permission. We got them to the ship and we had a seaplane crane, it was a seaplane tender we were on, and they just put a strap on them and lifted them up and set them down in the hold of the ship.

I rode it all over Japan. The only trouble I had was getting gas if I ran out off the base. I'd go to a little grocery store and mama-san would hang a hose out the window. It was about 70 octane gasoline, I didn't like to do that but I had to get back to base.

Cliff Majhor was a character, and a heckuva rider. He was also a dapper, handsome guy. He'd leave Merhar's around 7:00 pm with a woman, bring her back and at 8:00 pm he'd leave with a different woman. I don't know where they went.

Don Tindall was our hero here in Portland. His brother, Ronnie, was quite a bit bigger than Don, he was taller and heavier. Their father, Slick, was actually a Greyhound bus driver and he did house painting on the side. He was an old, old time motorcyclist. They used to go to Long Beach (Washington) before WWII and scream up and down the beach.

To this day I'm no hot shot motorcycle rider. I'd ride up there on Mt. Scott, and have a hard time going up the hills and coming down would scare the crap out of me. But then those crazy nuts started racing down the hill! No way would I ever do that! Just to come down a muddy hill you had to make damn sure that you never used your brakes. With a single cylinder motorcycle you just pull the compression release and let the thing roll. Don't touch the brake.

That's what made Donnie such a good road racer. He rode his motorcycle every day—that was his transportation. I never saw him in a car until many years later, when he was selling sports cars. He rode on these wet city streets, with rains, he lived in Sellwood. He'd been doing dumb stuff on the street. There at the last he had a Triumph Trophy with a Thunderbird engine in it. He'd do different crap and the cops would chase him and he'd never stop for a cop. He'd say screw you! He'd jump a curb and ride into Grant Park and the cops couldn't go after him. He knew different places to go and he could ditch a cop. He went into the Navy the same time I did and that was because the Portland police suggested he go into the service!

Riding Bike in the Fifties

Action at Benton Lane. Don 8W and Ron 36W Tindall exhibit beautiful racing form as they sweep out of a turn on their KHRM's.

Riding Bike in the Fifties

On Being the Wild One

No work at the garage/ things slow/ all cars running
so the wop boss says Drake take the afternoon off
which pisses me/ two years here at a buck an hour
I need that money / bills piling up/ things to buy
but happy too/ shuck off baggy floppy coveralls
slip into trim leathers/ sling my lunch bucket
around my shoulder/ fire the engine/ free

engine warm/ cruise easily across town
long before the rush-hour traffic/ open spaces
riding easy/ two school girls wave/ hi hi

near home/ turn off for Indian Rock
ease through Dwyer's mill/ up the straight road
searching the rocks from this distance for a glint
of chrome/ a fender/ another rider/ see nothing
but rocks/ cliffs/ trees/ the old stone quarry
shift down/ down/ cross the water-cut gulley
and follow the ruts/ headed up
stand on the pegs/ lean/ crank it on/ tire
spinning/ a short spurt across the clearing/ hit it
straight up for fifteen feet/ over the top
the bike off the ground/ way off/ coming down
back wheel first/ digging in/ back off/ lean left
drop/ then up the high hill/ a narrow rut going up
the bike bucking/ faltering/ catching
I'm in trouble alone/ broken leg/ broken head
but the bike sails over the top/ high/ turn sharp
or it's the other side/ rocks/ straight down
grab the compression release/ dead-stick it down
pomp/ pomp/ pomp/ keep off the brake or you're dead
back wheel sliding around/ crossed up
dead engine rolling faster/ at the bottom
let her go/ clear the carb/ and take off
head for the trials course/ take the lower trail
brush a blur on both sides/ eyes on the ground
crank it on/ leaning right/ left/ running at speed
brake/ switchback/ then go/ lay it down/ go
sweat running all over/ hard work/ lifting
and then you know: today everything's fine
the bike right at the thin margin
an inch from disaster/ but always within the latitudes
of speed/ faster/ imagining another bike in pursuit

Riding Bike in the Fifties

adrenalin up/ another motor churning/ passing
the sense of competition that drives you faster
faster than you thought possible/ no mistakes
leaning/ laying it down/ feet up/ knobby kicking dirt
and finally at the top/ alone/ engine throbbing
a giant pulse/ kill it/ the empty sounds of silence

below the trails/ rocks/ the mill/ the city
below people are working/ paying bills/ I'm alone/ free
I open the lunchbox/ two jelly sandwiches/ hot coffee
somehow it tastes better than at work/ I'm tired/ happy
O no journalist could know how it feels
flexing against T-shirt/ under leather/ to stomp
in heavy boots which are no weight/ to fly
to be young/ beautifully broke/ standing feet apart
under clear blue skies/ clean air/ the wind
riding a machine which uses so little gas and oil
you don't need to work/ the adventure of motion
moving into manhood/ under clear skies/ the world
an open endless hot horizon

mobile/ free/ moving   gone

Glenn Wright cutting a trail in the wilderness

Make the Whole Country Your Vacation Land!

HARLEY-DAVIDSON
HYDRA-GLIDE

REACH out-of-way fishing regions, hidden lakes and streams . . . travel picturesque back-country roads, breathtaking mountain trails . . . see America the scenic "out-in-the-open" way! It's easy and economical . . . on a Harley-Davidson Hydra-Glide. You ride swiftly and comfortably, too . . . float along like a breeze!

Going Down

I rode two wheel machines, motorcycles and scooters, for years, and went down only twice.

The first time was on my 1947 BSA 500cc. twin, a real suicide machine. I was young, and experience is a good teacher. I'd been riding long enough to feel I knew what I was doing, but not long enough to anticipate trouble or to be able to make corrections. I've heard stories about a car that turned left in front of a motorcycle, and the rider intentionally laid the bike down then remained on the bike. That's skillful riding! My experience has been that when things start to go wrong you're at the mercy of forward momentum and gravity. There are times when you can't do anything. Making incorrect repairs doesn't help either. I had replaced the throttle cable on that old twin and, dumb me, I put it on backwards, so I had to push the right grip forward rather than pull it toward me. There's a reason the cable pulls and that's so it will roll forward when the cable is released.

Rather than fix the cable correctly, I went out riding with two buddies that Saturday morning at Indian Rock. I managed to ride okay off the road, although it was unnatural to push the throttle forward. What should have been a reflex action required thought. Later we rode down to 82nd Avenue, a fairly busy four lane road. About two blocks north of Holgate we wanted to turn left and we stopped to wait for traffic. As usual, it was raining and the pavement was wet. John Farlow made a left turn on his Velocette, followed by Bob Kaseweter on his BSA single. A couple cars passed and it was my turn. I angled the wheel, leaned left and gave the bike a little gas. My BSA twin was always a little soft, a little slow to respond, and although it would run at 70mph it lacked that sharp crack, the immediate response I yearned for. In hindsight, it was probably that manageable speed which kept me out of trouble. What was funny about this situation was that I was stopped to turn, gave the bike a little gas, the rear tire kicked out from under me and suddenly I was free of the bike. I slid across two lanes of traffic at about 5 mph. There was nothing I could do. I was aware of cars coming toward me, and straight ahead I saw the approaching curb. It would've been a good time to have been wearing a crash helmet, but none of us did. I kept sliding, the cycle somewhere behind me; I wanted to cushion my head in my arms but I couldn't move them. Finally I came to a stop about a foot from the curb. I was wearing a heavy leather jacket, which saved me from some road rash, but as I started to get up, to go back and rescue my cycle, I noticed that both knees on my Levis were worn away.

I'm always curious about a wreck, and I always wonder whether there's anything to be learned, to avoid such an accident in the future. What gets me about that low speed mishap is how quickly it happened and how helpless I was. During a wreck there's a force that holds us immobile, or thrusts us forward, and, in my experience, makes any kind of voluntary movement impossible.

Going Down

The second accident happened about seven years later. I'd been riding all those years, so I had lots of experience, but when trouble hit all that experience didn't matter. In 1958 I bought a new Vespa scooter, the first one delivered in Portland, Oregon. I loved that machine! It was quick, quiet, maneuverable and terribly thrifty—I'd drive 150 miles on a tank of gas. It was beautifully made: that 150cc.two-stroke had only three moving parts, and the engine, three speed transmission and rear drive bolted together, eliminating the need for shaft drive or chains, which were always a problem on cycles. When I lived in Portland I rode that scooter at least thirty miles a day, rain or shine, from home to college to work and back home, and it never failed me. And I rode it hard. My motorcycle friends kidded me about riding a scooter, so I made it go. Looking back, I have to say that was not very smart. A Vespa has small wheels and you can't lean it into a corner the way you can motorcycle. If you get into trouble the scooter offers little protection. My accident of years earlier should have taught me a lesson about what can happen at 5 mph, but I didn't learn. I rode with the wild abandon of youth, eager to be going somewhere, even if it was nowhere important.

In the summer of 1961 my wife and I decided that we should ride the scooter from Eugene to Ashland, a distance of about 200 miles, and spend a week at the Shakespearean Festival. I had a luggage rack on the rear of the scooter, and we loaded our sleeping bags and knapsacks. We had a great time, horsing around during the day and seeing a different play each evening. At night we'd follow the Vespa's headlight beam up Lithia Creek, walking beside the scooter until we reached our camp in the woods. It was a fun vacation, and also inexpensive, which was important because, as usual, we had little money.

According to the owner's manual, that Vespa would top out at 49.5 mph. But the shop mechanic, a guy named Mario, who was from Italy, had milled the head and removed the muffler's innards, giving that scooter more zip. I ran it for hours at 55 mph. That's how fast we were travelling down the highway south of Eugene. We were enjoying the scenery and we were happy with life, except for those times when a Greyhound bus or a logging truck would ride our butt. The highway had not yet become I-5, an interstate freeway, and it was mostly two lane. Since we were running flat out 55 mph, and the speed limit was 70 mph, a truck would have to wait for a straight section to pass us. The drivers were angry, and gave a blast of their air horn as they passed.

At Azalea, the highway branched out, with a third lane added for traffic that passed under the highway, came up an approach and turned onto the highway, using that extra lane to gather speed and merge with southbound traffic. That traffic seemed to be primarily log trucks that had deposited a sheen of oil on the asphalt. When the scooter hit that oil the rear tire spun, the engine turned about 20,000 revs and it slowly slid out from under us. I immediately released the throttle but it was too late. Everything happened in slow motion. I simply held onto the handlebars as the scooter skidded along on its side. I have no idea how far it skidded but at the time it seemed to slide forever. When things stopped I was sitting in the middle of a lane of traffic, and my wife was down the road, getting to her feet. As usual, we did not have crash helmets. Neither of us was seriously hurt, nor was the scooter.

We rode on to Ashland, but upon our return a week later, at my wife's insistence, we took Highway 99, a slower two lane road. And the next year, when we bought a Lambretta scooter in Europe, she insisted that we buy crash helmets. She had learned something. I don't know that I had, but even now, 51 years later, I have dreams of a snorting log truck nudging the rear of our scooter as we started up that hill, and I have visions too terrible to contemplate.

Cruising on a Vespa at Midcentury

After nearly 50 years, I could be wrong, but I have long believed that I owned the first Vespa scooter delivered in Portland, Oregon.

In 1956-57 I worked at Cronin Company, an automotive warehouse at N.W. 10th and Flanders St. Sometime during that year, a Vespa dealership opened at 10th and West Burnside, on a pie-shaped piece of land across from the building which then housed Wentworth and Irwin, a Nash dealership, and which now houses Powell's City of Books (the world's largest bookstore according to *The Guinness Book of Records*). I drove past the Vespa dealership twice a day, and I could see the two or three scooters on display. What got me to stop was the Vespa with a sidecar that appeared one day; it was terribly cute, and I was impressed by the simplicity of the torsion bar suspension. I knew right then I wanted one.

I grew up at a time when scooters were practical transportation, because new cars were unavailable during World War II and hard to get for several years after the war. A store near my house, Foster Sporting Goods, had a row of new Servi-Cycles for sale, and occasionally I'd see a Whizzer motorbike, or a Doodlebug or a Hiawatha or Cushman scooter. I'd find a motorized scooter in the classified ads and I'd try to convince my father that I could use it on my paper route. I never got a scooter, but I spent a lot of time trying to figure out how I could adapt a small motor to my bicycle. When I turned 16 I built a hot rod, and after graduating from high school I had motorcycles, including a beautiful BSA Gold Star, which was sanitary and quick.

By 1957 I was moving away from cycles and hot rods. In the fall I began classes at Portland State College full-time, and I was thinking lofty thoughts and hanging out with a better class of people, so I abandoned my old ways. I bought a car coat, Ivy League pants with a little belt in the back, penny loafers, paisley shirts and V-neck sweaters. As I changed, so did the world. In Portland it became possible to buy beer by the pitcher and walk around in the tavern with a glass of beer and throw peanut shells on the floor, just like people did in the joints in 'Frisco. A coffeehouse opened near PSC, where Beatniks drank espresso, played chess and read *On The Road*.

In this kind of atmosphere, it seemed like a good idea to buy a Vespa scooter. Actually, I can't remember exactly why I bought one, but I know I was thinking of the larger world. I wanted to go to Europe. I wanted to enjoy things I'd read about in *Esquire* and *Playboy*, such as seeing a bullfight, eating gazpacho and paella, cruising the Riviera on two wheels and drinking the *vin du pays* of many countries. I wanted to wear a Harris tweed jacket with leather patches on the elbows, suck on a pipe and carry a slim black umbrella. On a more mundane level, the city was installing parking meters around the college and it was getting increasingly difficult to find a parking space for a car. Also, there was a ceramics professor at PSC, Ray Grimm, who rode a Vespa he'd bought in Italy, and he made the scooter sound like fun transportation.

Cruising on a Vespa at Midcentury

So, one day in the spring of 1958 I went to the dealership and bought a 1957 Vespa 150 for $250. It had been brought to Portland by the dealership's mechanic, used as a demonstrator, and was now fitted with a 1958 engine and titled as a 1958 model. The mechanic was Mario, and I remember that he had a sister, an attractive young woman with reddish-blonde hair, who took classes at PSC.

The scooter was in beautiful condition, and had a luggage rack, the only accessory. It was quick! I was told that the mechanic had milled the head to raise the compression and gutted the muffler to reduce back pressure. I never had the scooter apart, so I can't testify that those modifications had been done. But I do know that the scooter, although quiet, would run past 55 mph on the speedometer, 5.5 mph faster than the top speed stated in the owner's manual. I loved riding that Vespa! After the various problems I'd had with chains and sprockets on motorcycles, I admired the Vespa's engine/transmission/final drive construction, and the fact that the engine had only three moving parts! It seemed that the designers had thought of everything. The lights ran off the magneto, making a battery unnecessary. Below the seat was the fuel lever; when I ran out of gas, as I often did, I'd flip it over to the reserve level, which would always get me home, and later to a station.

On the left side of the body was a compartment that held the factory tool kit and tire pump, two-stroke oil and a measuring can, a couple rags, and other miscellaneous stuff—with room left over. Behind the seat was a pillion for an occasional passenger, and behind that was the optional luggage rack which would carry a decent load.

I could've got a spare tire, which bolted in place under the rack, but changing a tire was no problem. One Saturday morning, in a hurry to get to my job in a gas station, I found that the rear tire was flat. I laid the scooter on its side, and using a wrench that came with the scooter I removed the bolts that held the two-piece wheel together, cold-patched the tube, reassembled the wheel, pumped up the tire with the factory hand pump and was on my way in ten minutes.

The scooter was terribly inexpensive. Gas cost between 16¢ and 20¢ cents a gallon, and two stroke oil wasn't much. The mileage was around 150 miles on a full tank. A license plate was either $2.50 or $3.00 a year, and I never did have any insurance. I replaced the spark plug with some frequency. I rode that Vespa for five years, and the only expense, besides spark plugs, was a control cable and a new inner tube, the result of taking on a passenger without increasing the tire pressure, as per the manual. I never did any maintenance, other than washing the scooter—maybe I waxed it too. But the total cost of riding that Vespa for five years was around $25!

I had a lot of fun with that scooter. I met girls who just had to have a ride. I'd park it anywhere—between cars, on the grass, on the sidewalk. I'd park it in front of a funky-fashionable tavern like the Pink Bucket and enter wearing my car coat, Ivy League slacks and penny loafers, looking, I thought, very smooth.

I cruised from place to place all night, and when I came home, often very late, that scooter was so quiet my mother never woke up.

And yet, sometimes I look back, especially late at night, and wonder whether I should have owned that scooter. Sometimes, these nights, I stare into the darkness and celebrate the notion that I'm still alive. The problem was that I expected that Vespa to be two machines: a quiet, classy scooter that would get me around town in style, and a fast grand prix machine. I had ridden motorcycles for several years, and some of the bikers would get gas at the station where I worked. They'd always give me some guff, indicating that they considered the Vespa a toy. That was a reason for riding the scooter hard. I'd ride between rows of cars at a stop light, as I'd done on motor cycles, and when the light changed to green I'd grab a handful of throttle and run it through the gears, speed shifting. It seemed impossible to over-rev the engine, and so I kept it wound up.

It rains a lot in Portland, and while the leg shield kept my lower body dry, my upper body was quickly soaked. One morning, after a short ride, I was really wet, so I stopped at an army surplus store and bought a cloth coat with a snap-in alpaca liner. Rain could not penetrate that liner, and the coat, with the hood raised, gave me a sense of protection. Of course, I never wore a crash helmet. It scares me now when I think of leaving PSC, going up Broadway, then downhill, through a couple right turns, merging with traffic and then entering a left hand curve and heading over the Ross Island bridge, going as fast as I could. On a motorcycle I could just lay it over, but the smaller wheels on the scooter required a different kind of control, similar to certain kinds of skiing.

In 1959 I transferred to the University of Oregon and I took my Vespa with me. It was ideal transportation because my world had diminished to an area of about two square miles. It was a quick trip across campus, through the Pioneer Cemetery or into downtown Eugene. If I were in no hurry, I'd ride through the alleys that intersected almost every block, looking in people's back yards.

So if the Vespa was ideal transportation, why weren't there more? Actually, there weren't many bicycles either. I suspect that most college students considered scooters and bicycles as juvenile transportation. That's my impression, years later. The only other guy I knew at UO who had Vespa was Ed Nadeau, who I'd met at PSC. Ed also had a fairly new MGA roadster. He probably shouldn't have been driving or riding anything, because he got pretty drunk several times a week. He had plenty of family money, and during the summer of 1959 he rode his Vespa all the way to Mexico, an incredible journey. He wanted me to go with him, but, alas, I had to work.

In the fall I rented a room, the old dining room actually, one huge room in a Victorian house that had been converted into apartments for students during World War II. It was like a Charles Addams drawing, and therefore it attracted Beatniks, loners, outsiders, non-students and some really smart and creative students. My room cost $15 a month. After a few months I became manager, which meant I got the entire third floor in exchange for collecting rents and keeping people from destroying the place. Like Vespa riders, the renters were a distinct minority, and on occasion it was us versus the fraternity and sorority people.

One renter was Kernan Tumer, who went on to have a distinguished career with the Associated Press. He had a 1940s Cushman motor scooter. Today it would be lovingly restored, but in 1960 it was a clunky, noisy scooter with an old blue paint job that'd been put on with a brush. The difference between that Cushman and my Vespa was like night and day. One example, the Vespa shifted by rolling the handlebar grip, while on the Cushman you had to let go of the handlebar, reach down low on the right side and slide a lever forward.

Another renter was Brad Reed, an outdoorsman, who loved to boat, fish and climb mountains. He went on to become one of the first serious ski bums in Aspen. He showed up at the house one day with a brand new BSA Spitfire, a full-size cycle with a 250cc single cylinder motor, I think; it was supposed to be an economy bike, because it had things like a partial seat, with no room for a passenger. But it was a neat bike, with a blue tank and the BSA emblem. I think Brad's bike was the only example I've ever seen.

Then a couple, Garth and Virginia, rented a room. I can't remember the details, whether one showed up before the other or if they came together. I clearly remember that in 1960 it was unusual, even shocking, for an unmarried couple to live together. I don't think there was a law against it, it just didn't happen. They were the only couple to live together in unmarried bliss during the years I managed the joint. My own wife didn't move in with me until after we were married!

I believe Virginia got a Vespa before Garth did, or maybe they brought their Vespas when they moved in. Garth had a Vespa 150, similar to mine. Virginia, who worked for a delivery service, rode a Vespa Grand Sport, the only one I saw during those years. It had a 200cc motor, bigger tires and was taller than my Vespa. I don't think they took classes, but they had jobs and rode their Vespas rain or shine. Then one day on their lunch hour they rode their Vespas to city hall and got married. I hope it lasted.

In 1962 my wife and I headed for Europe, and I sold the Vespa to a German student in Eugene, Oregon for $195, a little less than I'd paid for it. We got to Europe, and in Roosendaal, Holland, I bought a used Lambretta scooter. I was told it was a 150cc but it turned out to be a 125cc model, which put us at a disadvantage in places like the Pyrenees. The two scooters were quite different, and because the Lambretta had shocks on both sides of the wheels and the engine in the center, I think it was the better scooter on a long journey, while the Vespa was better in town.

I've told myself many times that I'd like to have another Vespa, but only when the price of gas forces others to ride something with two wheels. Part of what saved me from disaster was that traffic was greatly reduced in those days. It's hard to explain, but look at photographs taken during the 1950s in a city like Portland, and unless the photographs were taken at rush hour, the streets are almost empty. That was also what made riding a scooter so fun.

Al Drake touring Europe on a 1955 Lambretta 125cc scooter.

Albert Drake on his 1967 BSA 441 Victor

About the Author

Albert Drake was born in Portland, Oregon when it was less populous and life had the quality of Norman Rockwell paintings. He was educated in public schools and followed his father's footsteps, working for years in service stations, garages and automotive warehouses. He eventually attended Portland State College, and got his degrees at the University of Oregon. He twice won the Ernest Haycox Prize for fiction. For nearly 30 years he labored in the groves of academe, where he was cited for his outstanding teaching and rose to the rank of Full Professor. He was the first academic to teach a class in science fiction as literature, and for several years he was Director of the Clarion Science Fiction Workshop. He has received numerous academic and creative grants, including two major grants from the National Endowment for the Arts. His fiction, poetry and prose have been widely published in literary quarterlies and popular magazines, including *Redbook*, *Epoch*, *North American Review* and *The Best American Short Stories*. He is currently Professor Emeritus of English.

Books by Albert Drake

Poetry
Michigan Signatures (Ed) (1969)
Riding Bike (1973)
Cheap Thrills (1975)
Roadsalt (1975)
Returning to Oregon (1975)
Garage (1981)
Homesick (1988)

Fiction
The Postcard Mysteries (1975)
Tillamook Burn (1977)
In the Time of Surveys (1978)
I Remember the Day James Dean Died (1983)

Novels
One Summer (1979)
Beyond the Pavement (1981)

Non-Fiction
Street Was Fun in '51 (1982)
The Big "Little GTO" Book (1982)
A 1950's Rod & Custom Builder's Wishbook (1985)
Herding Goats (1989)
Hot Rodder!: From Lakes to Street (1993)
Flat Out (1994)
'Fifties Flashback (1998)
Portland Pictorial: The 1950s (2006)
Northwest Oldtimers (2007)
Age of Hot Rods (2008)
Jacket & Plaque (2008)
Christmas at Ed's Richfield (2009)
Overtures to Motion (2011)

www.flatoutpress.com

www.ingramcontent.com/pod-product-compliance
Lightning Source LLC
Chambersburg PA
CBHW080515110426
42742CB00017B/3122